DISCOVERY

WITCHES & WIZARDS

Paul Dowswell

Consultant: Susan Greenwood

HERMES HOUSE

This edition is published by Hermes House

Hermes House is an imprint of Anness Publishing Ltd
Hermes House, 88–89 Blackfriars Road,
London SE1 8HA
tel. 020 7401 2077; fax 020 7633 9499;
info@anness.com

A CIP catalogue record for this book is available from
the British Library

Publisher: Joanna Lorenz
Managing Editor, Children's Books:
 Gilly Cameron Cooper
Editors: Lisa Miles, Louisa Somerville
Editorial Reader: Richard McGinlay
Series Design: John Jamieson
Designer: Margaret Sadler
Illustration: Peter Bull, Vanessa Card, Chris Forsey,
 Terry Gabbey, Guy Smith, Clive Spong
Picture Research: Veneta Bullen
Photography: John Freeman
Stylist: Melanie Williams

Anness Publishing would like to thank the following
children, and their parents, for modelling for this book:
Harriet Bartholomew, Alex Martin-Simons, Adrianne
Punzalan, Ben Rodden

PICTURE CREDITS

b=bottom, t=top, c=centre, l=left, r=right

AKG Photo: 5tl, 5bl, 8br, 8bl, 9tr, 9cl, 9bl, 11tr, 12br,
26br, 26bl, 31bl, 31tl, 34bl, 37br, 37tr; E.T Archive:
5br, 5b, 7tr, 10bl, 23tl, 23tr, 23bl, 30tr, 31tr, 31ct, 37tl,
45cl; 53tl; Bridgeman Art Library: 4br, 6b, 9cr, 13tl,
30bl, 44br; Dover publications: 5tr, 27tl, 27bl, 39c,
39bl, 52tl; Mary Evans Picture Library: 4bl, 12bl, 13tr,
15b, 15tr, 16bl, 19tl, 22bl, 22br, 23br, 23c, 38bl, 38br,
44bl, 45t, 52bl, 52br, 53br, 53tr, 53bl, 58br, 58bl;
Fortean Picture Library: 7tl, 15tl, 18bl, 27c, 31br, 36br,
36bl, 48bl, 49tl, 59tr, 59cl, 59bl; Werner Forman
Archive: 51tr; Ronald Grant Archive: 4tr, 54bl, 55tr,
55tl, 55bl, 55cr; The Kobal Collection: 54br; Peter
Newark's Historical Pictures: 13bl, 18br, 39tr, 42bl,
43tr, 43tl, 43br, 45b, 48tl, 49tr, 48br, 49c; Eye
Ubiquitous: 49br.

10 9 8 7 6 5 4 3 2 1

CONTENTS

Witches and Wizards................. 4

World of Magic.......................... 6

In Ancient Times....................... 8

Good Luck Charm............... 10

Medieval Magic.................... 12

Early Witch Hunts..........................14

Dress as a Witch 16

Animal Allies.................................... 18

Magical Decorations........................... 20

Magic Spells..................................... 22

Make a Charm Bag............................ 24

Secret Skills...................................... 26

A Witch Mobile.................................. 28

The Magic of Alchemy........................... 30

Magician at Work................................. 32

Dress as a Wizard............................ 34

Seeing the Future.................................. 36

The Sabbat.. 38

Make a Jack-o'-lantern............. 40

Witch Hunting...................... 42

Trial and Punishment............ 44

A Magic Seal......................... 46

Shamans and Magic 48

A Shaman's Mask........................... 50

Fairy-tale Magic............................ 52

Screen Witches............................. 54

A Hallowe'en Feast........................ 56

Modern Witchcraft........................ 58

Timeline..60

Glossary..62

Index...64

Witches and Wizards

Did witches and wizards ever really exist? Are they still around today? The answer to both questions is yes. Throughout history in every society, certain people have practised magic. That is, they have tried to make something good or bad happen by using spells and supernatural forces. We call these people witches, a word that often describes women who practise magic. Male witches may be called wizards or warlocks. Witches and wizards may also be called sorcerers, magicians, witch doctors or shamans, depending on the time and place that they came from. In many cultures today, magic is a thriving and valuable part of everyday life.

Some of the ideas we have about magic are based on fact, or on legend, but many are complete inventions. In Europe, in the period between 1450 and 1650, people were obsessed with witch hunting, an obsession created by the Christian church. Thousands of innocent people were arrested as witches, and then tortured and executed. Some truly believed they had magic powers while others were tortured into admitting things they did not do. This is the era from which many traditional images of witchcraft come.

▲ **HUBBLE BUBBLE**
Witches gather around a bubbling cauldron in the company of demons, to brew up an evil spell. This is how it was imagined that witches behaved. People suspected of being witches were once put to death in Europe. The photograph comes from the Swedish film, *Witchcraft Through the Ages*. It was made in 1922 and is still frightening viewing today. It is a silent horror movie that supposedly tells the story of witchcraft.

◀ **A PRIME SUSPECT**
Any poor old woman living alone with just animals for company would have been a prime suspect for being a witch in Early Modern Europe. Many villagers and townsfolk were convinced that witches were making evil magic (known as black magic) in their community. Even harmless village wise women, who told fortunes or made healing concoctions and love potions, were suspected of being witches. Although some of those accused may have been practising black magic, most suspects were completely harmless, and some may even have been mentally ill.

▲ **ENCHANTING SORCERESS**
Witches from myths and legends were not all sharp-faced old hags. Some were beautiful and beguiling young women, such as Morgan le Fay, seen here dressed in sumptuous silks and velvets, casting a magic spell. Morgan was a sorceress and enemy of the legendary King Arthur of Britain, who was supposed to have ruled around AD450. Like many witches from all times and cultures, Morgan was said to have had the power to fly.

▲ CONJURING UP MAGIC

A wizard summons magical forces to help him in his work. As he follows a complicated spell through to its climax, a ball of light containing magical letters appears before him. Men were called witches, as well as wizards and warlocks. These are male magicians or sorcerers who are supposed to have magic powers.

▲ JOIN THE CLUB

Witches gather together for a sabbat. This was a ceremony in which the Devil was supposed to be summoned and evil magic was done. The picture is entitled *Witches' Kitchen* and was painted by Hieronymus Francken, who lived from 1540 to 1610. At this time in Europe, fear of witchcraft was at its height. The women here are surrounded by ghoulish objects – a severed head, skulls, daggers, spell books and odd creatures.

▲ MAGIC AND SCIENCE

From the 1500s, people known as alchemists made half-magical and half-scientific experiments in an attempt to discover the legendary philosopher's stone. This was a substance which would enable them to turn ordinary metals into gold and guarantee eternal life. Alchemy was the forerunner of early chemical discoveries.

NORTH AMERICAN SHAMAN ▶

Clothed in wolfskin, this shaman is from the North American Blackfoot tribe. Holding a spear and a tambourine to assist his magic, he performs an elaborate ritual dance that will lead a dying man safely into the spirit world. Shamans and magical healers were important members of their communities. They cured the sick with specially chosen herbs, performed rituals and dances often in a trance-like state, chanted and said prayers that would bring good fortune to their people.

World of Magic

Throughout history, members of almost every human society have practised magic. From the windswept tip of South America to the baking plains of central Australia, wherever humans have set foot, magical beliefs have accompanied them. There is an amazing variety of magical practices and rituals, but all cultures seem to have a concept of good and bad, or white and black magic.

Many cultures have, or have had, magicians known as shamans. These people are sometimes also referred to as witch doctors or medicine men. A shaman can communicate with spirits and drive them away, or enlist their help in magic-making.

In the past, magic, and the people who practised it, were often treated differently in different parts of the world. For instance, for the tribal people of Kamchatka, in the far eastern reaches of Russia, magic was central to their lives. Their shaman was a healer, and an essential part of their society. In Europe, however, practitioners of magic, real or imagined, have often been outsiders, and been persecuted (punished for their beliefs).

NORTH AMERICA

◀ **TOTEM POLE**
This woodcarving shows a thunderbird, a magical creature worshipped by the Haida people of North America. The bird had wings that made thunder, and brought storms and rain to water the earth. The Haida tribe believed their shamans could control or pacify supernatural creatures.

Peru

MAGIC IN LIMA ▶
A pottery jar from Lima, Peru, shows a shaman of the Mochica culture. A spirit companion helps him to examine a sick woman. They are trying to understand the cause of her illness.

SOUTH AMERICA

ATLANTIC OCEAN

N

W   E

S

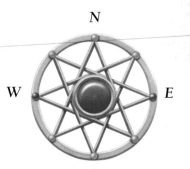

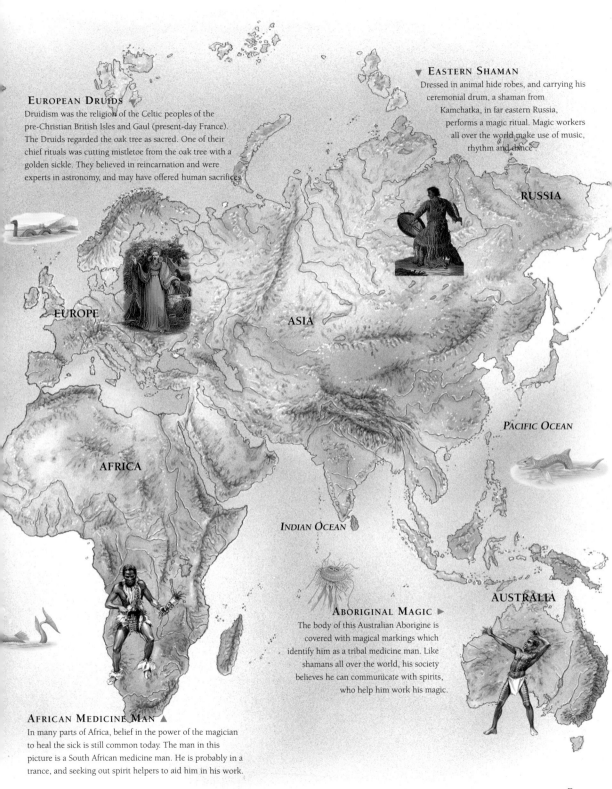

EUROPEAN DRUIDS

Druidism was the religion of the Celtic peoples of the pre-Christian British Isles and Gaul (present-day France). The Druids regarded the oak tree as sacred. One of their chief rituals was cutting mistletoe from the oak tree with a golden sickle. They believed in reincarnation and were experts in astronomy, and may have offered human sacrifices.

EUROPE

▼ **EASTERN SHAMAN**

Dressed in animal hide robes, and carrying his ceremonial drum, a shaman from Kamchatka, in far eastern Russia, performs a magic ritual. Magic workers all over the world make use of music, rhythm and dance.

RUSSIA

ASIA

AFRICA

PACIFIC OCEAN

INDIAN OCEAN

AUSTRALIA

ABORIGINAL MAGIC ▶

The body of this Australian Aborigine is covered with magical markings which identify him as a tribal medicine man. Like shamans all over the world, his society believes he can communicate with spirits, who help him work his magic.

AFRICAN MEDICINE MAN ▲

In many parts of Africa, belief in the power of the magician to heal the sick is still common today. The man in this picture is a South African medicine man. He is probably in a trance, and seeking out spirit helpers to aid him in his work.

7

In Ancient Times

From the start of human history, people have believed in the power to influence people and events by the use of supernatural forces. In Stone Age cave paintings of bison and horses more than 15,000 years old there are also drawings of strange, semi-human figures. Some archaeologists think these are witch doctors or shamans performing magic rituals. Ancient Egyptians, Greeks and Romans, too, all had beliefs and traditions that accepted magic as part of their everyday lives.

People may have feared sorcerers, for they knew they could practise both good and bad magic, but they also felt that they needed them. If they were ill or about to set out on a journey, magic spells and rituals were performed to please the gods and ask for their protection.

Over the centuries, the magic and myths of early civilizations were woven into European culture. People's ideas about witches were based on these ancient magicians and sorcerers, and on ideas put forward by the Christian Church during the witch-hunts of 1450-1650.

▲ STONE AGE MAGIC

Deep inside a cave, a Stone Age shaman, dressed in an antlered headdress, is leading a ritual to ensure that there will be plenty of game to hunt in the year ahead. Shamans were thought to have a direct link to the spirits. Their rituals were intended to ensure that the community was in touch with the spirits.

◄ EGYPTIAN BABOON GOD

Thoth, the ancient Egyptian god of the moon and wisdom, was believed to be the creator of arts, science and magic. Thoth is shown here as a baboon with a student at his feet. Like many magical creatures he could change his appearance. He is often shown as a man with the head of an ibis (a large bird). Shape-changing gods appear in several ancient myths, and this ability was also attributed to witches.

ANIMAL MAGIC ►

This ancient wall painting, half-man, half-animal, is known to some as the Dancing Sorcerer. It was discovered in a cave at Les Trois Frères in the French Pyrenees mountains. The figure has wolf's ears, stag's antlers, bear's paws and a horse's tail, and is thought to be a Stone Age shaman.

CIRCE AND HER PETS ►

According to legend, the wild animals surrounding the ancient Greek sorceress Circe were once men. Circe transformed them by means of a magic potion. The idea that witches could turn themselves and others into animals, and that they kept particular animals as servants, has its roots in the myths of ancient Greece and Rome.

WILD TIMES ▶

Half-dressed men and women, wild with excitement, dance
in a frenzy around Bacchus (called Dionysus in ancient
Greece). He was the god of wine and intoxicating herbs and
plants such as ivy and laurel. In ancient Greece and Rome,
Bacchus and other gods of pleasure and indulgence, such as
Pan, were worshipped in mysterious cult ceremonies. They
involved wild drinking, dancing and the sacrifice of animals.
How people imagined sabbats (witches' gatherings) was
directly inspired by ancient rituals such as these. At sabbats,
though, it was the devil who was centre of attention.

◀ FUTURE TRANCE

In ancient Greece an oracle was a
holy place where people could go to
ask the advice of the gods, through a
human interpreter. This scene takes
place at the site of the most famous
oracle in history, the shrine of the god
Apollo, in Delphi. His interpreter is a
priestess called the Pythia. She sits on
a great tripod and chews laurel
leaves. These contain a drug that
sends her into a trance, during which
she communicates with Apollo. The
priestess then predicts the fate of the
questioners. The ability to see into
the future has been a talent of
magicians throughout history.

▲ BLOOD AND GUTS

On the reverse of this Greek bronze mirror is
etched Chalenas the soothsayer (fortune teller).
Soothsayers, both male and female, were able to
predict future events by various methods such
as the examination of the internal organs of
sacrificed animals. The Greeks and Romans
were firm believers in the ability to see into the
future. Palm reading and astrology were both
popular in ancient Rome. Some soothsayers
used unusual techniques such as reading the
movements of clouds and birds.

◀ HORNED GOD

This human-like image of Cernunnos, the Celtic deer god, was
engraved on a silver cauldron around 100BC. Often, as here, the
god is shown surrounded by animals, suggesting that he has
special powers over them. Like the Greek god Pan, Cernunnos
had horns. These horns made a reappearance in Christian images
of the Devil, whom witches were said to worship and obey.

Good Luck Charm

An amulet is a magic charm that people wear or carry to protect them against evil spells. They have been worn since ancient times and are supposed to bring good luck to the wearer.

The amulet in this project is based on an ancient Egyptian design. It features a symbol called an *udjat*, which represents the eye of the sky god Horus. Amulets of this type became especially popular around 1000BC. A gold amulet would only have been worn by the Pharaohs (kings) of Egypt, since gold was thought to be the flesh of the sun. This privilege was later extended to priests and nobles.

> **You will need:** *felt-tipped pen, ruler, corrugated cardboard, scissors, masking tape, a few teaspoons of plain flour, water for mixing, mixing bowl, metal spoon, newspaper, chopping board, fine sandpaper, sheet of paper, fine paintbrushes, bright blue, dark blue, gold, black and white acrylic paints, pencil, coloured foil sweet wrappers, PVA glue, glue brush.*

A bright blue stone has been carved into the shape of a scarab beetle and polished to make an amulet (magic charm). It is from ancient Egypt and more than 3,000 years old. Amulets were placed on the chest of an embalmed corpse (preserved with oils and spices) to represent the heart. A dead person's heart was removed and embalmed separately. The amulets were believed to protect dead people in the next world. The scarab beetle represented the sky god, Horus, and was sacred to the Egyptians. The base of this amulet is covered in hieroglyphs (Egyptian writing). On either side are udjat eye symbols. Udjat means healing or protection, and symbolizes the god Horus' eye, which was torn out by his murderous uncle, Seth. Thousands of udjat amulets have been found wrapped up in Egyptian mummies.

1 Use a ruler to measure out and draw a rectangle on the piece of corrugated cardboard. The rectangle should measure about 24cm x 6cm.

2 This is for the basic bracelet shape. Cut neatly around the edges of the rectangle you have drawn, using the pair of scissors.

6 Leave the amulet to dry completely. Then gently rub it with fine sandpaper to smooth the surfaces. Place a sheet of paper underneath to catch the rubbings.

7 Paint the amulet all over in a bright colour, such as light blue. If possible, use acrylic paint, because it is slightly water-resistant and will not smudge.

10 Cut some brightly coloured foil sweet wrappers into 1cm strips. Snip each strip across to form lots of 1cm squares.

11 Using PVA glue and a fine glue brush, carefully stick the foil squares around the top and bottom borders of the amulet. Leave to dry completely.

3 Bend the card around to form a bracelet shape. (You could try it on now to make sure it fits.) Overlap the edges slightly and fasten them with masking tape.

4 Put some flour in a bowl. Slowly add water, stirring as you go, until you have made a thick paste. Then tear up strips of newspaper.

5 Now work on a chopping board. Dip strips of the newspaper into the paste. Cover the amulet inside and out with about 3 layers of papier-mâché.

This is the top and bottom of a heart-shaped scarab amulet, which is also around 3,000 years old. The writing on the underside asks the amulet (which represents the dead person's heart) not to say bad things against its owner when he is judged by the gods in the afterlife.

Your finished amulet makes a striking piece of jewellery. In Ancient Egyptian times the amulet would have been worn by a king or noble and made of precious stones such as blue lapis lazuli set into solid gold. It would have brought fine health and good luck.

8 When the paint is dry, use a pencil to draw a design on it. You could copy the eye of Horus, as shown here, or make up your own Egyptian-theme design.

9 Continue your pattern all the way around your amulet. For the border design, draw lines around the top and bottom of the amulet 1cm from the edges.

12 Use a fine paintbrush and gold, dark blue, black and white paints to colour in the pencil design on the amulet. Leave to dry.

13 Use more gold paint to decorate inside your amulet. Make sure the paint is completely dry before you wear the amulet.

Medieval Magic

▲ A DEAL WITH THE DEVIL

The Greek monk Theophilus is about to accept a written contract, or pact, being pressed on him by a fearsome-looking Devil. According to legend, Theophilus, with the help of a sorcerer, sold his soul to the Devil during the AD500s. However, he then had second thoughts and was eventually able to regain his soul. This tale became the inspiration for one of the most famous pacts in literary history. The plot was used as the basis for *Dr Faustus*, a play by Elizabethan dramatist Christopher Marlowe. In the play, a scholar sells his soul to the Devil in exchange for supernatural powers and extended youth. As witchcraft hysteria took hold of Europe, the story became mixed with other myths, and people suspected all witches of making a similar pact.

I n pre-Christian Europe, most people believed in not just one god, but many gods. Christianity and the teachings of Jesus spread throughout the Roman Empire, and in AD313 became the official religion. This brought great changes to everyday life. In AD476, the Empire fell when western Europe was overrun by the Visigoths, barbarian tribes from Germany. Europe entered an unsettled 600-year period often called the Dark Ages. During this time, the Christian Church was about the only unchanging element in people's lives.

People still believed that some men and women could cure disease and make love potions. However, they also feared that the same individuals had darker powers, such as causing crops to fail, or bringing illness and death upon their enemies. In the Middle Ages (1050–1450), the Church wanted to stamp out such beliefs. They were called heretical because they did not fit in with the Church's teachings.

◄ MEPHISTOPHELES

Thirteen centuries after the original tale, the myth of selling souls to the Devil was still worth telling. This illustration from the 1800s shows Dr Faustus with Mephistopheles, who was sent by the Devil to be Faustus' servant. Marlowe's play *Dr Faustus* is still performed today.

SATANIC ARISTOCRAT ►

One of the most notorious sorcerers of the Middle Ages was the Frenchman Gilles de Rais. Born into an aristocratic family in 1404, he was reputed to live more lavishly than the king. Seeking new ways to finance his luxurious lifestyle, he took to alchemy, in the hope of turning ordinary metals into gold. He also developed an interest in Devil worship, and intended to persuade the Devil to help him gain greater wealth and power. He was reported to have kidnapped and killed 140 children for black magic rituals.

GOD AND MAGIC ▶

Albertus Magnus (1193–1280) was the bishop of
Ratisbon in Germany and a student of magic,
alchemy and philosophy. At that time monasteries
and cathedrals were great centres of learning, and
churchmen were some of the most educated and
open-minded men of their day. Many were
interested in investigating all that
science, magic and religion had to
offer. Before hysteria about witchcraft
took hold in Europe, many churchmen
saw little wrong with the study and
even the practice of magic.

◀ JEALOUS WITCHCRAFT

King Henry II of England kept his
beautiful mistress, Rosamund, hidden
in a secret room in one of his houses.
During his rule (1154–1189) he banned anyone from his court who
practised magic. His wife Queen Eleanor, however, was said to have secretly
been a witch. She found out about Rosamund and was jealous of her.
Eleanor discovered where she was hiding by following a thread that led to
her room. She then offered Rosamund a poisoned drink, which killed her.

◀ FRENCH HEROINE

The French heroine, Joan of
Arc rides in front of her
followers, wearing white
armour. She is going to meet
the heir to the French throne,
later Charles VII. Joan was the
daughter of a poor farmer. At
the age of 16 she claimed to
have heard the voices of saints
and angels urging her to drive
the English out of France. She
persuaded King Charles to let
her command a force against
them. Her victories inspired
the French, but she was
captured and put on trial by
the English. They accused her
of heresy (opposing the beliefs
held by the Church). The
charges against her included
keeping company with devils.
She was burned at the stake at
Rouen in France, in 1431.

Early Witch Hunts

From 1450 to 1650, fear of witches was widespread in Europe. Witches, real or imagined, were persecuted in what the Church saw as an all-out war between good and evil. The vast majority of the accused were unfortunate innocents.

Anti-witch hysteria was increased by publications such as the *Malleus Maleficarum* (Hammer of Witches) in 1486 and the *Compendium Maleficarum* (Handbook of Witches) of 1626. These books set out rules for detecting witchcraft and were very prejudiced against women. The contents were based upon the imagination of the writers or the confessions of torture victims, and shaped people's views of how witches behaved.

Fierce religious struggles as Protestants broke away from the Church in Rome, encouraged an obsession with witchcraft – witch hunts were used to get rid of opponents. From 1580, the number of trials rocketed.

▲ IMPRISONED!

Chained to a cold cell wall, with her hands tied above her head, a bewildered woman awaits her fate. The fear felt by those arrested and imprisoned for witchcraft can hardly be imagined. Unless they freely confessed to being a witch, suspects were often tortured until they did so. Courts were not allowed to pass sentence without such a confession, but anyone successfully convicted of witchcraft faced execution.

◄ HOMAGE TO SATAN

Sitting on an ornate wooden throne, in an isolated countryside location, the Devil instructs witches in the secret art of black magic. It is not just women who have come to listen. Several of those gathered before him are men. The way the Devil is depicted, with a horned goat's head on the body of a man, scaly bat wings and taloned feet, is typical of the time. This illustration and the one below are taken from *Compendium Maleficarum*.

REJECTING GOD ►

Witches and wizards queue up to pay their respects to the Devil. They trample on the cross, the most sacred symbol of Christianity. People believed that witches conducted ceremonies that mocked the Christian religion. This was at a time when Protestants were rebelling against the rule of the Catholic Church in Rome. The Church authorities often accused people who did not go along with their ideas, of witchcraft.

▲ EVIL TRICKS

Demonic creatures circle in the sky above, while the Devil instructs four old women in the dark art of making waxen images, or hex dolls. People believed that not only did witches ally themselves with the Devil, but they were also taught black arts by him. This woodcut from around 1680 shows a widely believed aspect of witchcraft. Wax or wooden images of a person were made in order to work evil magic upon them. It was thought that if the doll was deformed or destroyed, then injury or death would befall the person it resembled.

◀ BROUGHT BACK FROM THE DEAD

Magician Edward Kelly summons a corpse from the grave in Lancashire, England. In many cultures, witches and wizards are said to be able to raise the dead, and European witches were no exception. Kelly was a friend of Queen Elizabeth I's royal astronomer, Dr John Dee. Kelly liked people to believe that he was an alchemist and that he had other magical powers, too. If such a scene as the one shown here ever took place, it was no doubt performed with a great deal of trickery.

UP BEFORE THE KING ▲

James I, who ruled England and Scotland from 1603 to 1625, showed no mercy to people condemned of witchcraft. He was fascinated by the supernatural and wrote a book called *Demonology*. It was an account full of extraordinary stories based on little more than gossip, rumour, and confessions that were extracted through torture. James wrote it following an alleged attempt on his life by a group of men and women known as the North Berwick witches. These are the people who are shown cowering before him in the picture.

◀ TAKING TO THE SKIES

A gaggle of witches, with black robes and pointed hats circles an isolated country church, some of them on broomsticks. This engraving is taken from Victorian writer Sir Walter Scott's *Letters on Demonology and Witchcraft*. It was used to illustrate a story about the North Berwick witches. Deserted graveyards were supposed to be favoured locations for witches to cast their spells.

Dress as a Witch

This project will show you how to create the familiar image of a witch, dressed in ragged clothes with a broomstick. You could also paint on a wrinkly, warty face and black teeth. This appearance developed from a much feared figure from folklore – the hag. Myths and legends from ancient Egypt through to pre-Christian Europe concern ugly old women who were said to use demonic powers to bring misfortune to those around them. Tragically, in the days of witch persecution, many poor, old women looked like the hags of folklore and became obvious targets for witch hunts.

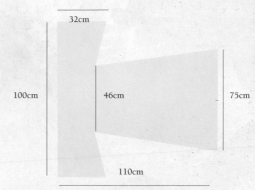

1 Using a pencil and ruler, copy the above template on to some scrap paper, such as old newspaper.

> **You will need:** *pencil, ruler, scrap paper, black cotton fabric 200cm x 110cm, white pencil, scissors, needle, sewing thread, newspaper, stiff paintbrush, silver paint, A2 sheet of thin black card, sticky tape, black card 32cm x 32cm, silver card, PVA glue, glue brush, green and black tissue paper.*

This fairy-tale illustration from the 1800s by Kate Greenaway has all the classic features we have come to expect in a witch. She hovers before us, broomstick in hand, her shabby cloak billowing in the light of the full moon.

6 Lay the dress on newspaper. Dip the brush in silver paint. Pull the bristles back towards you to spray paint on to the fabric. When dry, spray the other side.

7 Roll a piece of thin, black A2-sized card into a cone shape. Use white pencil to draw a line on the card to show where it overlaps and should be taped.

11 Cut around the outside of the ring. Cut out the centre, leaving an extra 3cm inside the ring. Make snips into the ring, as far as the inner line.

12 Fit the hat rim on to the bottom of the hat. Use sticky tape to fix the tabs that you snipped in the rim to the inside of the hat.

2 Fold the black fabric in half lengthways. Lay it out on a flat surface. Use the template to draw the witch's dress shape on the fabric with white pencil.

3 Cut the dress shape out. Cut a slit 24cm across in the middle of the folded edge, for your neck. Cut a second line 12cm long down the back of the fabric.

4 Turn the fabric inside out. Use a needle and sewing thread to do a simple running stitch up each side and under the arms of the witch's dress.

5 Cut a jagged edge along the cuffs of each sleeve and along the bottom of the dress. Turn the dress inside out (so that the fabric is right side out).

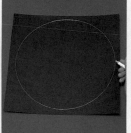

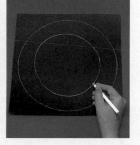

8 Cut away the excess card. Roll the card back into a cone shape and secure with sticky tape. Trim the bottom edge of the cone to fit your head.

9 Place the hat on a piece of black card about 32cm square. Using a white pencil, measure and draw a circle around the hat rim, but 5cm away from it.

10 Use a white pencil to draw a second circle around the hat, this time close to the rim. You should now have a ring 5cm wide.

Complete your witchy look with face paints. Paint dark lines under your eyes and around your mouth to make you look as if you have wrinkles. You could also colour one of your teeth with black lip liner. You will also need a broom, which you can make by tying twigs to a old broom handle or long piece of thick dowelling.

13 Draw a rectangular shape for a hat buckle on to silver card. Draw a second rectangle inside the first one. Cut out the buckle and glue it on.

14 Cut green and black tissue paper into long strips for the witch's hair. Glue the strips to the inside of the hat, except at the front.

17

Animal Allies

▲ **FLY GUYS**
A witch stirs her magic brew, simmering in the cauldron, while watched by her fly familiars. Many different kinds of animals were thought to be familiars. Ferrets, spiders, rabbits and even hedgehogs were all cited in witchcraft trials.

▲ **OWL COMPANIONS**
This elaborate engraving from the 1800s shows a witch preparing a spell. Her owl familiar hovers above, keeping watch, no doubt, for any meddling intruders. The owl's huge staring eyes, sinister hoot, eerily silent flight, and night-time existence, have long made it a creature associated with witchcraft. The Latin name for owl, *strix*, was the same word given to a witch.

The eerie hooting of owls, cats screeching, toads croaking in the darkness of night – are all the noises what they seem or could they be something more sinister? For many people who lived in Europe around the 1600s, animal sounds floating through the night air made them think that evil lurked outside their doors.

Some animals, particularly cats, toads and owls, were thought to be associated with witches and wizards and were called familiars. They were said by the Christian Church to be demons who had taken on animal shapes and assisted witches and wizards in their work. The reward for an animal's services was blood, either as a pinprick drop from the owner's finger, or taken from a sacrificed animal.

Familiars apparently could make themselves invisible and change from one animal into another. When a witch was accused and imprisoned, she would be secretly watched. If any animal came near her, even a fly, this would be used as proof that she was a witch receiving her familiars.

Witches' cauldrons traditionally contained a toad, a creature that people believed witches often changed into. People spat or threw a stone if they saw a toad to avoid bad luck.

FELINE ACCOMPLICE ▶
Cats, particularly black ones, were thought to be the most common witches' companions. They were said to bring gifts such as flocks of sheep, or perform evil deeds such as murder, for their human owners. Cat familiars were given eerie names – Pyewacket, Grizel and Prickeare are mentioned in accounts of witch trials. Usually caught and tried along with their mistresses, they invariably met the same grisly fate. Fears that all cats were familiars sometimes led to entire cat massacres in Early Modern towns or villages.

▲ A GIFT FROM SATAN

Satan, shown here in the middle, offers a familiar to a witch. The fierce-looking beast is unlike any real animal, but its sharp talons, muscular build, long thick tail and the heavy chain used to hold it, all suggest a creature of lethal power. This woodcut appeared in an English book, called *The Kingdom of Darkness,* published in 1688, which supposedly exposed the practice of witchcraft.

▲ WHAT'S IN THE POT?

A host of grotesque familiars attend a witches' sabbat. They gather around hopefully, as if expecting to be fed from the cauldron. This engraving depicts sinister goings-on in England in 1612. Like the strange black creature in the picture above right, many of these familiars are unlike any known animal. One has a dog's body and face, but human arms and legs. Another one has a bat's face and dog's body.

◄ GALLOWS MENAGERIE

This gruesome scene commemorates the hanging of the so-called Chelmsford witches. It appeared in a lurid pamphlet giving details of the case, published in 1589. It accused the women of "devilish practices and keeping of spirits" – a reference to the animals that supposedly helped them perform their witchcraft. In the foreground is one of the accused witches, Joan Prentice, who also hangs on the gallows behind. She is surrounded by several toads and a couple of monkeys. Her familiar stands on her lap to lick her face.

◄ DANCING TOADS

Toads are frequently mentioned as witches' companions. Their warty skin and love of damp hiding places has long made them seem sinister creatures to humans. As well as helping a witch in her work, toads were also a handy source of ingredients for magic potions. A lotion made of toad spit, for example, was said to make a witch invisible. Witches were supposed to take great care of their familiars. The two toads in this illustration have been dressed in velvet capes with little bells, and taught to dance.

Magical Decorations

Particular symbols and letters are said to have magical powers. You could use the shapes and symbols in these projects to make great decorations for a Hallowe'en party. Either make a frieze around the room where you are holding the party, or hang them in the window. You could also make black silhouettes of cauldrons, broomsticks and pointed witches' hats for your party decorations.

Hallowe'en is celebrated on October 31st. It is an old European festival marking the start of winter. Many present-day witches believe it is the time when communication with the dead is possible. The astrological symbols shown in the first project are associated with magic. Each symbol represents a particular star sign. Astrology (the study of the planets and stars) is often used in an attempt to foretell the future, as in horoscopes. Black cats are often associated with witches, as they were thought to be familiars.

For the astrological symbol you will need: black card, ruler, plastic dish, white pencil, small pot, scissors, white and gold acrylic paint, paintbrush, PVA glue, glue brush, tissue paper, sparkly string.

For the cat frieze you will need: sheet of black paper, ruler, scissors, white pencil, PVA glue, glue brush, sheet of paper, glitter.

1 Take a piece of black card measuring about 15cm square. Place a slightly smaller dish on the card and draw around it with a white pencil.

2 Carefully place a smaller pot in the centre of the white circle. Draw around it. You will now have two white circles, one inside the other.

1 Above is the template for the cat frieze. Cut out a piece of black paper about 25cm x 100cm. Fold the paper in half widthways, then fold it in half again. Make sure the edges are firmly creased.

3 Using a white pencil, draw the cat shape provided on to the paper. The face, a front paw, a back paw and the curl of the tail must touch the edge of the paper.

4 Carefully cut around the cat through the layers of paper. Take care not to cut around the parts of the cat that are touching the edges.

5 Very carefully unfold the cat frieze. You should end up with four cats that are joined head to head, tail to tail and paw to paw.

6 Lay the cat frieze down on your work surface. With a glue brush, dab a little glue where each cat's eyes should be and on the tips of the paws.

3 Cut around the circles to make a hoop shape. Draw around the dish and pot again on to another piece of black card. Cut out a second hoop shape.

4 Decorate the hoops with splatters of gold and white paint. When dry, dab glue on to the back of one hoop. Stick it to a sheet of coloured tissue paper.

5 Turn the tissue paper over. Make a loop to hang up your symbol by folding a strip of black card in half and gluing to the top. Glue the second hoop in place.

6 Use scissors to trim the tissue around the edge of the hoop. Cut a star sign from black card and glue it in the middle. Tie sparkly string to the loop.

2 Unfold the paper. Lay the paper flat with the short end towards you. Then fold the paper up again, like a concertina, along the creases.

STAR SIGNS

♑ Capricorn	♉ Taurus	♍ Virgo
♒ Aquarius	♊ Gemini	♎ Libra
♓ Pisces	♋ Cancer	♏ Scorpio
♈ Aries	♌ Leo	♐ Sagittarius

7 Place a sheet of paper underneath the cats. Sprinkle glitter over the eyes and paws and shake off the excess. Leave the cats to dry.

Your black cat frieze makes a striking decoration for any spooky party. You will need to make several friezes in different colours to fit them around the walls of a room. Use the same idea (a concertina-fold and a large piece of paper) to make other frieze designs, such as owls and pumpkins.

Magic Spells

"Eye of newt, and toe of frog; wool of bat, and
tongue of dog; adder's fork, and blind-worm's sting;
lizard's leg, and howlet's wing".

These are some of the grisly ingredients which are listed
in a spell recited by the three witches in the famous play
Macbeth, by William Shakespeare. Spells were an essential
part of a witch's work and were spoken or written down in
an attempt to influence people or events.

There were a great many different types of spells. Good ones promoted
such things as healing, fertility and long life. Bad ones caused illness,
failure and even death. Many spells had long been practised by village wise
men and women who provided villagers with ancient remedies for
illnesses and other afflictions.

During the time when witches were persecuted, natural healers were no
longer able to openly continue their work. However, spells from ancient
times survive in the modern world in herbal remedies, in which the
ingredients can have good effects on health.

▲ SECRET RECIPE
Reaching down to pluck another ingredient for a
spell, a witch hurries about her work under
cover of darkness. Many spells not only required
the right plants, but also specified the time of day
or night that they were to be picked. The moon
has always had magical associations. Plants
picked under the moonlight were thought to
have special powers.

◄ HUMAN INGREDIENT
Human remains have long been seen as a
powerful ingredient in spells, as this ghoulish
engraving from the 1800s shows. An English
witch called Mother Chattox has ordered a
servant to dig up a body. This will provide a
gruesome ingredient for a spell she plans to
work on the hex doll that she carries.
Fortunately for the local people, a good citizen
lurking behind a tree has spotted her and she
will soon be punished. The account of this event
dates from 1612, so it is almost certainly just a
story to spread bad feeling against witches.

RAISING A STORM ►
Two witches prepare a spell around a boiling
cauldron. As one adds a snake, the other plunges a
cockerel into the bubbling water. They are making a spell
to raise a storm, and in the sky above them a seething mass
of clouds spits hailstones. In Cornwall, England, people believed
witches were hired by smugglers or pirates to raise storms. The storms would
drive ships on to the rocks, where their cargo could be stolen.

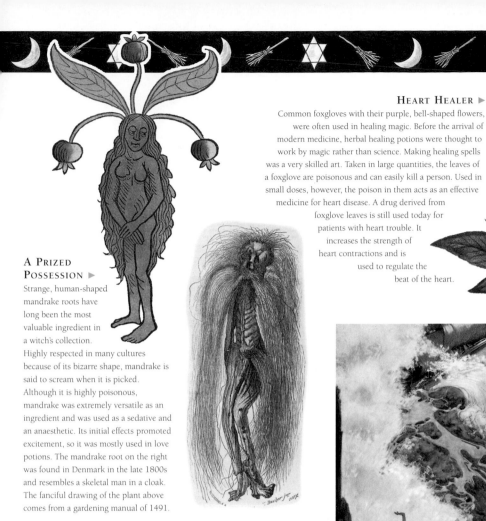

HEART HEALER ▶

Common foxgloves with their purple, bell-shaped flowers, were often used in healing magic. Before the arrival of modern medicine, herbal healing potions were thought to work by magic rather than science. Making healing spells was a very skilled art. Taken in large quantities, the leaves of a foxglove are poisonous and can easily kill a person. Used in small doses, however, the poison in them acts as an effective medicine for heart disease. A drug derived from foxglove leaves is still used today for patients with heart trouble. It increases the strength of heart contractions and is used to regulate the beat of the heart.

A PRIZED POSSESSION ▶

Strange, human-shaped mandrake roots have long been the most valuable ingredient in a witch's collection. Highly respected in many cultures because of its bizarre shape, mandrake is said to scream when it is picked. Although it is highly poisonous, mandrake was extremely versatile as an ingredient and was used as a sedative and an anaesthetic. Its initial effects promoted excitement, so it was mostly used in love potions. The mandrake root on the right was found in Denmark in the late 1800s and resembles a skeletal man in a cloak. The fanciful drawing of the plant above comes from a gardening manual of 1491.

◀ LOVE POTION

Frequently associated with romance and beauty, the rose was an ingredient in many love potions. Using techniques similar to those of perfume makers, witches would sometimes distil the rose oil in an effort to catch the very essence of the flower's captivating qualities. Many spells were woven to entice a reluctant man or woman to fall in love. Plants including the mandrake, periwinkle and even salad leaves, such as the endive lettuce, were also said to be suitable ingredients for such spells.

▲ STORM IN A CAULDRON

A ragged witch raises a storm, dancing on the edge of a cliff top beside a bubbling cauldron. She intends to drive a nearby ship to its destruction on the rocks. According to legend, witches could help seafarers, too. One spell sold to sailors enabled them to lock up the wind in a series of elaborate knots. When the ship was becalmed, the knots could be untied and the wind released.

Make a Charm Bag

To cast a spell is to make a particular kind of magic for a specific purpose. All spells require a specific ritual with a series of actions that have to be performed in a certain way and at a chosen time. They also require ingredients, such as plants, stones, feathers or soil.

A charm bag can be used to store a magical spell or to put crystals and other precious things in. This charm bag can be filled in a variety of ways. To help you to sleep well, put a little amethyst in the bag with a few sprigs of peppermint or some dried peppermint leaves. You could write a wish on a piece of paper. Fold it up and put it into the charm bag with some leaves from a willow tree. The willow tree is believed to help your dreams come true.

You will need: *dark blue velvet fabric, ruler, scissors, silver embroidery thread, large needle, pins, ordinary needle, dark blue sewing thread, silver cord, crystals.*

1 Take a large piece of dark blue velvet. Lay it out flat, reverse side up. Use a ruler to measure out a piece 30cm x 23cm and cut it out.

2 Take a length of silver embroidery thread and thread it through a fairly large needle. Make a knot at the end of the thread.

5 Bring the needle through from the back of the fabric again, in the position shown. Push the needle back down into the fabric to create a cross.

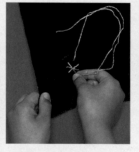

6 Repeat these big stitches several more times to create a star, as shown. Finish off at the back of the fabric. Cut the thread and tie a knot.

7 Sew more stars all along the bottom edge of the fabric. You could make them all the same size or make some smaller ones, too.

Put whichever crystal you feel you need into your pouch and keep it under your pillow. For example, turquoise is for good luck, rutilated quartz for happiness in love, and smoky quartz is for protection from bad atmospheres.

10 Fold the open end of the bag down. Fold it down again, so that there is no raw edge. Use pins to secure along the edge.

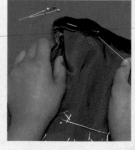

11 Use the needle and blue sewing thread to sew all around the edge of the bag. Use a running stitch again. Turn the bag the right way out.

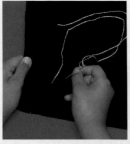

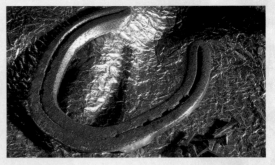

3 Turn the velvet over, so it is right side up. Push the needle and thread through from the back of the fabric in one corner as shown.

4 Push the needle and thread back through the fabric about 2cm diagonally away from where it came out. You have now made one large stitch.

Horseshoes are supposed to cast a protective spell over a house. They are made of iron, which is said to repel evil spirits. Reputedly, a horseshoe hung pointing down will protect against witchcraft, and a horseshoe hung pointing up will act as a good luck charm.

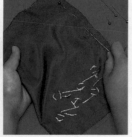

8 With the right side of the velvet up, fold the fabric in half widthwise. Pin together along the edge leaving the top edge opposite the stars open.

9 Thread an ordinary needle with blue sewing thread. Knot the end of the thread. Sew along the bottom and the side of the bag, using a running stitch.

Crystals come in many different shapes and colours. They are magical objects that are said to be able to focus energy and are often used in healing rituals today. Fill your charm bag with crystals that you think are particularly beautiful.

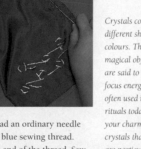

12 Tie a knot in each end of a length of silver cord. Sew the middle of the cord to the side of the bag, about 4cm down from the top.

13 Make sure the cord is fixed firmly to the side of the bag. Now put some crystals or lucky charms into your bag. Wrap the cord around to close it.

Secret Skills

The magical powers attributed to witches and wizards have much in common all over the world. According to myths and legends from many cultures, they can fly, shape-shift (change their shape) and make themselves invisible. So great was the fear of witchcraft, that many ordinary people invented the most extraordinary and ridiculous stories about witches. Sorcerers and magicians also believed that they could do such things through their spells and potions. The sensation of flying, for example, could be achieved by taking mind-altering substances such as poisonous mushrooms. A witch might have remained firmly on the ground, but in a trance, she would imagine herself to be spinning and weaving through the night sky at breathtaking speed. Shape-shifting could also be explained in this way. A witch in a drug-induced state could imagine herself to be any animal she wanted. At first, the Church was not prepared to believe that witches could fly, become invisible, or turn into animals. Such actions were explained as illusions created by the Devil, rather than authentic magic. Later, the Church saw witches as capable of all sorts of magical activities.

▲ FADING AWAY

A witch fades into her surroundings after swallowing a magic potion to take on the cloak of invisibility. Spells found in books show that becoming invisible was a complicated business. One spell required seven black beans, a dead man's head and an elaborate ritual to be followed over nine days. If the spell worked, the witch placed one of the beans in her mouth to become invisible. The instructions warn her not to swallow it, as taking the bean from her mouth was the only way to become visible again.

FLYING BROOMSTICKS ▶

These French illustrations from the 1400s are thought to be the first ever of witches on their broomsticks. Why the idea of a witch on a broomstick became so popular is something of a mystery. Although the image became common in illustrations of witches around this time, confessions used as evidence in witch trials rarely mention them.

HAGS INTO HARES ▶

In Europe, witches were said to disguise themselves as hares, and go about stealing milk from cows, or spreading illness to other farm animals. Stories were told of farmers who had trapped or shot at a hare, only to see it change back into an old hag before their eyes. This hare was drawn by Albrecht Dürer (1471–1528), a German artist of the period.

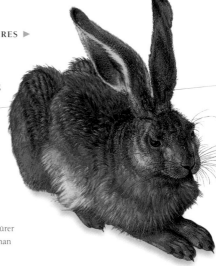

◄ FLY-FASTER OINTMENT

Broomstick at the ready, a young witch prepares to take to the night sky. Her accomplice, a ragged, pointed-faced old woman, is rubbing flying ointment over her body. Such ointments were supposed to be made from the fat of human babies, plus herbs and drugs. Mandrake root was linked with flying, probably because of its mind-altering effects.

CAUGHT IN THE ACT ►

Unaware of a nosy neighbour watching them, four witches prepare to fly to a sabbat (a witches' gathering). Witches were thought to have rubbed ointment in their bodies to enable them to fly. Seen from left to right in the picture, one prepares her broom, one rubs in flying ointment, one shoots up the chimney and the last is already in the air. The illustration appears in a French book published in 1579.

▲ FLYING SHAPE-SHIFTERS

Three shape-shifting witches take to the air as a hailstorm brews. One has a donkey's head, one has a chicken's head and the other has a dog's head. This woodcut, taken from a German book published in 1489, may be the first illustration to show witches flying. Unusually, it shows the witches astride a branch rather than a broomstick.

◄ LEARNING THE MAGIC

This Italian woodcut depicts a scene from *The Golden Ass* by the ancient Roman writer, Apuleius. As her servant looks on, a witch begins to sprout feathers as she transforms herself into an owl. As she changes shape, she hides the magic ointment that has brought about this transformation in a cupboard. Apuleius watches from the other side of the door. He hopes to learn how the magic is done, but when he tries, he becomes an ass instead of an owl!

A Witch Mobile

In the days of witch hunts, around 1450 to 1650, people really did believe that witches could fly. Many woodcuts and illustrated manuscripts from the period show them doing this. Sometimes they are carried by demons, sometimes they sit astride branches, but most of the time they straddle brooms.

At certain times of the year such as Hallowe'en, when witches were supposed to be out in force, church bells would be rung throughout the night. It was believed that the sound of the bells had the power to stop the witches flying overhead.

Here you can make your very own mobile to depict a group of witches flying through the night sky, heading for their lair.

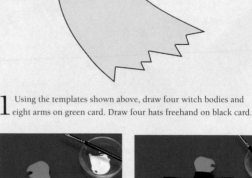

1 Using the templates shown above, draw four witch bodies and eight arms on green card. Draw four hats freehand on black card.

You will need: *pencil, thin green, black and white card, scissors, ruler, hay, four kebab sticks trimmed to 24cm, twine, PVA glue, glue brush, eight pieces of black felt 15cm x 15cm, eight pieces of black felt 8cm x 8cm, black felt-tipped pen, gold and silver acrylic paint, paintbrush, two pieces of 0.5cm dowel 40cm long, needle, sewing thread.*

4 Spread glue on one side of a witch body (except the head). Press it on to a large square of black felt. Repeat with the other three bodies. Leave to dry.

5 Trim the felt around each witch body. Glue a broomstick across each witch body at an angle, as shown. Leave to dry.

6 Spread glue on the remaining green side (except the head) of a witch. Press on to another black felt square and trim. Repeat with the other three witches.

10 Glue two hat shapes on to each witch's head. Using a black felt-tipped pen draw details such as eyes, spots and warts on each witch's face.

11 Paint the stars gold on each side and paint the moon silver on each side. Paint the two pieces of thin dowel gold. Leave to dry.

12 Cross the two pieces of dowel over at the centre and secure with twine. Leave a long piece of twine to hang the mobile up by and trim.

13 Thread a needle with sewing thread and make a knot in the end. Pass the needle through the top of a hat, but not too near the top, or it may rip.

2 Carefully cut out all the witch bodies, arms and hat shapes. Draw four stars and a crescent moon on white card and cut them out, too.

3 Trim a small bunch of hay into a bundle about 8cm long. Tie the hay around the end of a kebab stick with twine. Repeat with three other sticks.

7 Glue each arm (but not the fingers) on to a small felt square. Make sure you glue one side of four of the arms and the other side of the rest.

8 Leave the arms to dry. Then glue a pair of arms on to each witch. Leave to dry again. Now you are ready to make the witches' hair.

9 Cut two bits of green card 5cm x 2.5cm. Make cuts into them lengthwise, leaving a 1cm strip at the end uncut. Glue in place. Repeat for each witch.

14 Trim the thread, leaving quite a long piece attached to the hat. Repeat for the other three. Tie the other end of the thread to the ends of the dowels.

15 Attach threads to the stars in the same way. Tie them between the witches and the middle of the mobile. Tie the moon to the centre cross bar.

By hanging up the witches, stars and moon at different heights you will make your mobile more interesting to look at. Don't be scared if it starts moving in the night!

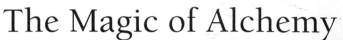

The Magic of Alchemy

Alchemy was an ancient art, half-magic and half-science. One of its major aims was to turn base (low value) common metals, such as copper, lead, zinc and tin, into precious metals such as silver and gold. No alchemist ever succeeded in doing this, but through their experiments they discovered much about the way materials reacted together. Their work was to lay the foundations of the modern science of chemistry. Alchemy first began in China and Egypt around 300BC. By the AD700s, alchemical ideas had spread to the Middle East, and reached Europe by the Middle Ages.

As part of their experiments, alchemists used spells and magical symbols to help them achieve their goals. They were deeply concerned for their souls, and their work had religious aspects. They had a motto, *"Ars totum requirit hominem"* (the art requires the whole man). It reflected their belief that through their work they could also perfect themselves as human beings.

▲ DANGEROUS WORK

This Italian painting, by Giovanni Stradano, depicts an alchemist's laboratory around 1570. The alchemist himself is seated to the right of the picture and is wearing a hat, a fur-lined coat and glasses. His text book open beside him, he directs his assistants in their complex tasks. An alchemist's workshop must have been an extremely dangerous place to work, with its fragile pots and jars, open fires and red-hot metals. After centuries of experimentation, alchemists never did succeed in changing base metal into silver or gold, but they did work out how to make use of many chemicals.

◄ GHOSTLY GLOW

German alchemist Hennig Brand falls to his knees in wonder at the pale luminous glow coming from inside a glass flask. Joseph Wright's painting of 1771 depicts Brand's workshop, bathed in the eerie light of burning phosphorus. Brand accidentally discovered the chemical phosphorus in 1669 while mixing together other substances. Many alchemists made vital discoveries such as this, and many of the pioneers of modern science took a deep interest in alchemy.

▲ ECCENTRIC PATRON

The eccentric Holy Roman Emperor Rudolf II was a great supporter of alchemy, especially in Prague in eastern Europe, where he kept his court. He also encouraged other scientists and astronomers in their work. He had a deep fascination for anything strange and unusual, and almost certainly suffered from some form of mental illness. In 1590, he commissioned the Italian artist Guiseppe Archimboldo to paint his portrait in the form of a collection of fruit and vegetables.

▲ MEDICAL PIONEER

One of the most famous alchemists was a Swiss physician known as Paracelsus, who lived from 1493 to 1541. He was well known as a medical pioneer. His pioneering ideas included using chemistry in medicine, the first clear descriptions of particular diseases, and an understanding of how immunization worked. He travelled widely in the Middle East and searched for an undiscovered element that he believed could change base metal into gold and be a cure-all medicine.

▲ SCIENTIFIC GENIUS

Sir Isaac Newton, who lived from 1642 to 1727, was perhaps the greatest scientist of his age. He made important discoveries in optics and motion that remain central to physics today. Like many learned men of his era he took a great interest in alchemy. He followed alchemist experiments, and made reams of notes on the subject. He also contributed his own original ideas to alchemical theories on the make-up of different substances.

◄ THE PHILOSOPHER'S STONE

An elaborate painting from the alchemist text-book *Splendor Solis* shows black, red and white birds inside a glass flask. The birds symbolize the chemical elements mercury, sulphur and salt. It was believed that combining these three elements in an alchemical process would produce the philosopher's stone – a substance that would transform ordinary metals into pure gold. Alchemists were also preoccupied with searching for the elixir of life, a chemical substance that would give eternal youth.

BIZARRE BEAST ►

This bizarre creature is made up of a human head and legs, a lion's mane, reptilian scaly skin, dragon wings and wriggling serpents' tails. It is the alchemist symbol Azoth and represents the essence of the element mercury. Alchemists were fascinated by mercury, which is a liquid, silvery metal. They were convinced it had special properties that would be vital to their work. This illustration is taken from an alchemist text called *Practica* by Paracelsus, which was first published in 1529.

Magician at Work

Here you can see what a magician's workshop may have looked like in the early 1500s. This was an era of great excitement in Europe, known as the Renaissance (meaning rebirth). New ideas about art, science and medicine were becoming popular. The continents of North and South America had recently been reached by Europeans. To learned people, the world seemed to be brimming with new possibilities.

For some wealthy people, magic and alchemy were areas open to investigation, but both were forbidden arts. Those who practised them risked persecution as heretics. A laboratory or workshop would have to be somewhere away from prying eyes, such as this basement below an ordinary shop in a town street.

By day, the magician runs a simple apothecary (drug shop) selling herbs, spices, lotions and potions to heal and help people. By night, and unknown to the townspeople, he practises his forbidden art and makes his spells, conjuring and creating by candlelight in the cellar of his shop.

◀ **MAGICAL MATERIALS**
The magician's assistant fetches more equipment and materials for a magical experiment. He has to be careful, as some of the ingredients are rare and fragile. The wizard is about to create a spell. He wants to unlock the secrets of materials such as mercury, sulphur, salt, or even ordinary water. Maybe he will be able to turn them into something much more valuable, such as gold or precious jewels.

KEY
1 *magician*
2 *magician's assistant*
3 *astrological chart*
4 *telescope*
5 *crystal ball*
6 *pestle and mortar*
7 *apothecary's shop sign*
8 *stairs to shop*
9 *metal stirring rod*
10 *boiling flask*

▲ NEW WORLDS

The magician is intensely interested in the world around him, distant places and the stars and planets beyond the Earth. He collects anything from foreign lands, especially from the newly discovered Americas. His pet monkey is his latest acquisition. It has been brought by ship from Central America.

◀ MIXING IT UP

The magician and his assistant are busy concocting their experiment. They are trying to turn iron into gold by melting, mixing and burning different chemicals. By day, the customers in the shop upstairs sometimes wonder where all the heat is coming from. Little do they know of the fires burning away below.

▲ WONDROUS WORKS

The magician's world revolves around the study of strangely mysterious books. His motto is "*Obscurum per obscurius, ignotum per ignotius!*" (The obscure is to be explained by the more obscure, the unknown by the more unknown.) His books are packed with weird and wonderful symbols and illustrations. These big, leather-bound, gold-embossed volumes have been handwritten over the centuries by old masters of magical arts. The magician adds his own spells and formulas to one of the books. Pausing for thought, he then carefully inscribes the magical symbols of his craft, using a fine quill pen.

Dress as a Wizard

Our image of wizards, like that of witches, is based on fairy tales and myths. Many stories concerning wizards date from medieval times, so their appearance is shaped by what people wore at that time. Wizards are also associated with alchemists who were often well-educated and rich members of society, which is why they are often pictured wearing sumptuous velvets and furs.

Wizards have never attracted the same hostility as witches. They are seen as mysterious magic workers, and as wise, rather than ugly and evil. This shows how women have been treated unfairly.

You will need: scissors, ruler, red silky fabric, pins, needle, red sewing thread, red wool, large safety pin, newspaper, silver fabric paint, fine paint brush, pencil, silver card, PVA glue and brush, silver glitter, small safety pins, sticky tape, pair of compasses or cup, 1cm dowel 35cm long, red tissue paper, red card 60cm x 60cm, black felt-tipped pen, thin elastic.

With his spell book in hand a wizard prepares to make magic, clothed in flowing robes covered in mysterious symbols. Wizards have always inspired fascination rather than fear, and have usually been associated with good magic rather than evil magic.

1 Cut a piece of red silky fabric measuring 160cm x 130cm. Pin the edges on the two short sides and one long side to make a hem. Then sew along the hem.

2 Cut two arm holes 15cm x 4cm in the fabric 35cm in from the shorter sides and 25cm in from the unsewn edge. Pin around the arm hole edges.

7 Spread newspaper on your work surface, then lay the cloak over it. Use silver fabric paint and a fine brush to make swirls on the cloak, as shown.

8 To make a fastener for the cloak, draw a star shape on silver card and cut it out. Glue glitter around the edges. Make three or four fasteners.

9 When the glue is dry, tape a small safety pin to the back of each fastener. When your cloak is on, pin them in place to hold the edges of it together.

12 Now glue the second star on to the first star, on the same side as the dowel. Make sure that the points of the two stars join up.

13 Roll the red card into a cone shape. Use a black felt-tipped pen to mark where it should be cut to get rid of the excess card. Unroll the cone.

14 Cut the card along the marked line. Roll up again and fasten with sticky tape. Trim the bottom of the cone so that it will fit on your head.

3 Make sure that the sides of the slits are pinned back on the same side of the fabric as the edges you have already sewn. Sew around the edges of the slits.

4 Fold the long unsewn edge of the fabric over about 4cm deep. Pin the fabric in position and then sew. This makes a drawstring tube for the neck.

5 Cut 30 pieces of red wool, each 140cm long. Knot at one end. Divide the threads into bunches of ten and plait them. Tie a knot at the end of the plait.

6 Ask an adult to secure a large safety pin through one of the knots. Use the safety pin to pull the knotted plait all the way through the neck tube.

Wizards in myths and legends are often pictured as wise old men. Finish your wizardly outfit with a long white beard made of cotton wool or white foam.

10 Draw a circle, about 8cm in diameter, on to silver card. Use compasses or draw around a cup. Draw triangles around it to make a star pattern. Cut out two stars.

11 Paint a length of dowel silver. When dry, glue the dowel to the back of one of the stars. Cut tissue paper into long thin strips and glue them on too.

15 Decorate the hat to match your cloak, by painting it all over with silver swirls. Paint different types of swirls to make the design look more interesting.

16 Make a chin strap by making two small holes on each side of the hat using a pencil. Thread elastic through the holes and tie.

Seeing the Future

▲ INSIDE A CRYSTAL BALL

A witch peers into a crystal ball and an image is revealed to her. While performing a fortune-telling, a scryer was thought to go into a trance. Images of future events only she could see would appear from the swirling mist inside the crystal ball. Perhaps she would see a shipwreck, a marriage, or even a murder. Predicting the future was a very inexact art. Fortune-tellers were said to need a great deal of practice to interpret visions.

Scrying (forecasting the future) was a skill supposedly practised by witches and wizards throughout the ages. Before the great witch hunts, a village wise woman or man would have been consulted about the future. The term scrying comes from an old English word *descry*, which means 'to make out dimly'. This is a good description of how most tellings were performed. The scryer would stare into a blackened cauldron full of water, or a still pond on a moonlit night, and go into a trance. Fleeting, blurry images were said to appear. Sometimes they would be actual events and sometimes they would be symbols that would need to be interpreted.

There were a great many ways of foretelling future events. Most common of all was astrology, a way of predicting the future via the movements of the stars and planets. Another way was palm reading, which involved interpreting the lines on the palms of a person's hands. How different playing cards fell or were dealt could also tell a person's future.

▲ GLASS FUTURES

Crystal balls are still used for scrying to this day. The best crystals for scrying are said to be those made of semi-precious stone, such as beryl, a green or white mineral found in granite. Although crystal balls are frequently associated with fortune-telling, they were not widely used in the past. They were heavy to carry around and expensive to buy. Witches who lived by the sea would make use of glass fishing floats, which were said to do the job just as well.

▲ A DARK REFLECTION

A magician in the dead of night summons spirits to help him see into the future with the aid of a vast, elaborate magic mirror. As well as good souls wafting down from heaven, the magician also appears to have called up demons and damned souls from hell. Mirrors have always been thought to have magic powers, and they could be used to see into the future. Dark mirrors, which are less reflective than ordinary mirrors, are said to be particularly effective.

◀ PALM READER

How to tell the future from the lines on a person's hand is said to be one of the oldest witchcraft skills. Palm reading in one form or another has been practised in India and China since 3000BC. At one time it was considered, like astrology, to be a science. It was even tolerated by the Church. However, so many tricksters claimed they had the ability to read palms that the Church condemned this custom at the end of the 1400s. Even so, palm reading has remained a popular attraction at fairs and markets right up to the present day.

▲ CARDS OF FORTUNE

A Dutch painting from the 1500s shows a fortune-teller laying out cards before a customer. Each card has a meaning. For example, the two of hearts signifies new friendships, the two of diamonds means trouble is brewing, and the ace of spades (the most feared card of all) signifies death. Using playing cards to see into the future was one of the most popular means of scrying.

▲ LOOKING AHEAD

The witch Anne Bodenham is fortune-telling with the aid of several demonic imps, a cat and dog familiar, and a magic circle drawn on the earth. This illustration is from Nathaniel Crouch's anti-witchcraft book, *The Kingdom of Darkness*, published in 1688. Bodenham stares into a seething cauldron of fire, spell book in hand. Behind her waits an accomplice, eager to see what the future holds.

NOSTRADAMUS ▶

The French physician Nostradamus, who lived from 1503 to 1566, is perhaps the most famous astrologer in history. He wrote two collections of prophesies known as *Centuries*. His predictions, which were written in a series of rhymes, still attract a great deal of interest today. Some people believe Nostradamus predicted future events such as the rise and fall of Napoleon and Hitler, and the assassinations of the American President John F Kennedy. Others feel that his obscure, enigmatic verses can be interpreted in different ways. They can mean anything the reader wants them to mean.

The Sabbat

It was said by the Christian Church that at certain times of the year, groups of witches would leave their homes and meet in far away places. The tops of mountains, windswept moors, or deep in the darkest woods, were all likely venues far away from the prying eyes of ordinary folk.

Once gathered together the witches would celebrate before their master, the Devil himself. These gatherings were called sabbats, a word based on sabbath, the Jewish and Christian holy day. It may be that the word sabbat came to be used because in Europe, during the Middle Ages, many people feared and disliked the Jews.

Sabbats were also supposed to include grotesque mockeries of the services of the Christian Church. Reports of such gatherings inflamed (strengthened) anti-witch hysteria in Europe. Town dwellers and peasants alike listened with fascination and repulsion to tales of demonic conduct. Most historians, however, believe that the whole concept of the sabbat, like many other aspects of witchcraft, was invented by the Church in order to control heresy.

▲ DANCING IN THE DARK

On a windswept autumnal evening, witches and warlocks dance themselves into a frenzy around a blazing bonfire. It was believed that wild actions such as this were intended to create a suitable atmosphere for the Devil, the sabbat's principal guest, to appear. It was believed that child sacrifices, wild parties and evil magic spells were performed at the sabbat, where no form of behaviour was too appalling. When the Devil did appear, he would scratch each attendant with his claw, causing a mark on their skin. Any blemish on the skin was known to witch hunters as the Devil's Mark.

▲ DEVIL'S FOOD

Devils and witches feast together at a banquet during a sabbat. As they eat and talk, a host of devil servants brings freshly cooked food from two roaring bonfires. The food at sabbats tasted foul, according to accounts given at witch trials. Salt was forbidden because witches hated salt, and rumours told that even babies were eaten at these occasions. This woodcut is from *Compendium Maleficarum (Handbook of Witches)*.

ANCIENT ROOTS ▶

Witch hunters may have got many of their ideas about sabbats from ancient myths and rites (rituals). Many ancient works of art show Greeks cavorting (dancing) with gods such as Dionysus and Pan, who were known for wild parties. In this illustration, dated around 1600, the dancers and demons are circling in a frenzy around a horned goat god. The goat is Satan rather than the more playful but mischievous Pan. Behind the revellers stands the silhouette of a gallows. This is a foreboding sign of the punishment to come when their demonic dabblings are finally discovered.

◄ THREE HEADS

A witch bows down to worship a bizarre three-headed demon. This illustration from 1544 shows that various witch stories became muddled in the telling, as they passed from one scaremonger to another. This demon seems to be a shape-shifter – a creature that can turn itself into different forms. However, instead of turning into just one half-animal form, it has taken on the heads of a lion, an eagle and a snake – all of which have long been regarded as dangerous and powerful creatures.

▲ GARLANDS FOR THE DEVIL

The supposed high point of any sabbat was the appearance of the Devil himself, most often in the guise of an animal. A goat was said to be Satan's favourite form, but sometimes the evil one would appear as a cat or even a toad. In this disturbing image by renowned Spanish artist Francisco Goya (1746–1828), the goat-devil has his horns garlanded with flowers. Around him, witches offer up starving children. Behind, on the left, is a grotesque collection of hanging hex dolls, which were used to throw curses upon victims. Goya was the court painter to the king of Spain. As he grew older he spent more time creating scenes of fantasy and terror rather than portraits. At the time, Spain was occupied by France. Many of Goya's paintings reflected this difficult political situation.

► ▼ A PRETTY UGLY PAIR

These two bizarre creatures are supposed to be devils. The grisly looking creature with horns and long taloned feet below is Belphegor. According to the Bible, Belphegor was an evil demon worshipped by the Moabites, enemies of the Israelites. The obese elephant-like demon is called Behemoth and was a Biblical demon of animal strength. Demons were supposed to be fallen angels who became servants of the Devil. Their job was to tempt human beings away from God and into evil ways. Witches were said to meet with them regularly and entertain them at sabbats.

WITCHES' PROPS ►

These are some of the props used to perform acts of evil magic. The severed hand has been hacked from the corpse of a hanged man. Known as a Hand of Glory, it was used to hold candles, or burned as part of an ingredient in a spell. A sheep's heart studded with nails was another common prop. A hex doll would have been used to direct evil magic at a particular person.

Make a Jack-o'-lantern

Hallowe'en, on October 31st, marks the old European festival of Samhain, which celebrated the start of winter, and was a time for remembering the dead. People celebrate Hallowe'en for fun, and make eerie hollowed-out pumpkins for the occasion. The face on the pumpkin represents a lost soul, with its hollow eyes and toothy grin. Such supernatural creatures have various names. They are called jack-o'-lanterns in the USA, will-o'-the-wisps in England, and foxfires in Ireland. It is said that they usually show themselves as glowing balls of light, which is why the pumpkin is lit from the inside. Here are two projects that show you how to make lanterns for an evening party.

For the jam jar lantern you will need: large jam jar, ruler, white pencil, thin black card, scissors, coloured tissue paper, PVA glue, brush, sticky tape, thin wire, wire-cutters, pliers, night-light candle.

For the pumpkin lantern you will need: a large and a small pumpkin, sharp knife, ice-cream scoop or large spoon, black felt-tipped pen, night-light candle.

1 Measure the height and circumference of the jam jar. Add 2cm for overlap. Use a white pencil to draw the rectangular shape on to thin black card.

2 Cut out the shape. Use the white pencil to draw a pattern of diamonds on the rectangle. Very carefully, cut the diamonds out.

1 Take the pumpkin and ask an adult to cut a 'lid' off the top using a sharp kitchen knife. Make sure that the top comes off in one piece.

2 Use an ice-cream scoop or a large spoon to remove and discard the insides of the pumpkin. You will need to scrape away quite hard.

Place a night-light candle inside the jar and ask an adult to light it for you with a match. Your jam-jar lantern will give out a dimly coloured glow.

5 Look at your pumpkin's face to see if you need to add more features. You could cut out a nose or eyebrows, or some more crooked teeth.

6 Take the smaller pumpkin and ask an adult to cut off the top, as before. Again, scoop out and discard the insides of the pumpkin.

3 Cut lots of different coloured tissue into squares big enough to fit over the diamonds. Glue the tissue squares over the holes and leave to dry.

4 When the glue is thoroughly dry, wrap the decorated paper around the jam jar with the glued side facing in. Seal the overlap with sticky tape.

5 Cut some wire slightly longer than fits around the neck of the jar. Twist the ends together. Cut some longer wire. Twist it around the first wire, as shown.

6 Loop the wire handle over the top of the jar. Ask an adult to help tighten up the neck piece by twisting the wire with a pair of pliers.

Once you have made a traditional jack-o'-lantern with a crude face, you could also try using other patterns. Stars and curly lines make good shapes. As with the jam-jar lantern, when your jack-o'-lantern is finished, ask an adult to light it for you with a firelighter.

3 Use a black felt-tipped pen to draw a spooky face on the pumpkin. Draw triangles for the eyes. Draw a large grin with lots of pointed teeth.

4 Ask an adult to use a sharp knife to cut away the eyes and the mouth. Push the cut-away shapes inwards, then pick them out and discard.

7 Using a black felt-tipped pen, draw a pattern of shapes on to the pumpkin to make a crown. Copy the shapes shown here, or make up your own.

8 Ask an adult to cut away the pattern. Put a night-light candle inside the large pumpkin, and then put the small pumpkin on top of the big one.

Witch Hunting

"Thou shalt not suffer a witch to live." So reads a passage in the Old Testament. Rarely has a verse in the Bible been so harshly used to justify such appalling cruelty. Over 250 years, from 1450 to 1700, hundreds of thousands of people were accused of witchcraft.

Nowhere in Europe was free of this persecution, which swept across the continent like a plague. It flared up in one country, then died down, only to burst out again in another. Anyone could be a suspect – priests or laymen, merchants or beggars, men or women – but most of all women. Although thousands of men were accused of witchcraft, it was overwhelmingly women who were burned at the stake or hanged from the gallows as punishment.

Some of those arrested probably practised some form of magic, but most witch hunt victims had nothing to do with witchcraft at all. Witch-hunting mania often erupted in a region following crop failure, disease or war. The local population were desperate to vent their anger and frustration on anyone they could find. It was also used by the Christian Church for the control of heresy. However, most of those sent to their deaths were simply old, eccentric or confused.

▲ Weighing a Witch

In order to prove a suspect guilty, witch hunters devised a series of bizarre tests. Weighing a witch was one of these tests. It was based on the logic that as witches could fly, they must be very light. The test varied from area to area. In some towns a suspect would be weighed against a heavy Bible, or against a set weight that she had to equal. Either way, a guilty verdict was almost guaranteed. This image of a witch trial in the 1600s shows the weighing scales at Oudewater in the Netherlands. The suspect, wearing the lightest of gowns, was first searched for any hidden weights, to make sure she was not trying to be heavier than she was. Then she was weighed.

◀ Public Humiliation

In the USA in 1692, an outbreak of witch hunting erupted in Salem, Massachusetts. This painting by American artist T H Matteson shows a suspect in the Salem witch trials undergoing the humiliating search for the Devil's Mark. Blemishes such as moles or scars were said to have been left on a witch by the Devil's claws or teeth. Two people faint in horror as a couple of meddlesome matrons point to the supposed blemishes of the accused girl.

◀ **UNDER ARREST**

A frail old woman is arrested for witchcraft, surrounded by six armed men. Her haggard, stooped appearance and ragged clothes tally with what many people at the time expected a witch to look like. This illustration comes from an account of the Salem witch trials in Massachusetts. The witch-hunting outbreak was caused when a group of young girls accused other villagers of witchcraft. It may have begun as a prank, but 141 people were arrested, and 20 were executed.

▲ **TRIAL BY WATER**

Another test for witchcraft was to be thrown into a river. If the suspect sank then she was innocent. If she floated, she was being rejected by the water as an evil witch. In this English woodcut of 1613, suspect Mary Sutton is going through this ordeal. Unusually, she is fastened to a rope held by two men, who will save her from drowning should the river prove her innocent.

THE WITCHFINDER GENERAL ▶

Matthew Hopkins questions two witches surrounded by their familiars. Hopkins was England's most famous witch hunter and even called himself the Witchfinder General. He scoured the counties of eastern England from 1645 to 1646, seeking out victims. He was paid for each arrest, and made a profitable living before he was discredited as a fraud and forced to retire. Torture was forbidden by English law, so Hopkins chose swimming, pricking tests and depriving people of sleep to force confessions from his victims. During Hopkins' search, more women were hanged for witchcraft in a year than they had been over the previous 100 years.

PRICKING STICKS ▶

One telltale sign for witchcraft was supposed to be an area on the body where the witch felt no pain. A suspect was stripped and poked all over with a sharp implement, called a pricking stick. This collection of pricking sticks includes one which has a blade, like a theatrical dagger, which would retract harmlessly into the handle if pressed against someone. Some witch hunters used pricking sticks like this, so as to be sure of condemning their victims. A witchfinder could stick this in a suspect and draw no blood and claim that she felt no pain. These were seen as clear signs that she possessed demonic powers.

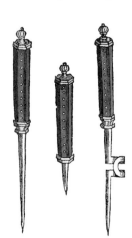

Trial and Punishment

Once sufficient evidence had been gathered to convince the authorities that a suspect was a witch, a grisly process of trial and punishment was set in motion. A successful prosecution (accusation of criminal action) depended on the suspect admitting that he or she was guilty. Most of them were probably completely bewildered by the charges, but were all too aware that death was the punishment if they were found guilty. Therefore, suspects were not likely to confess unless forced to do so. This was sometimes done by torturing them until they admitted whatever it was that their accusers wanted them to say.

Before about 1450 there were no witch trials. This was because people were not often accused of witchcraft and also because the law made prosecution difficult. A private individual was allowed to bring a case to court, but if the accused was found not guilty, then the accuser would be severely punished. As the Church became more concerned with stamping out heresy, the law was changed, and the Church or the Government acted as both prosecutor and judge. A confession extracted through torture was enough evidence to send victims to their deaths.

▲ INSTRUMENTS OF TORTURE

A frightening collection of torture equipment and tools of execution was used at the Bamberg witch trials in Germany in the 1600s. Among the items are a stake, gallows, executioner's sword, stocks, thumbscrews and a pillory. Such devices were blessed by a priest before they were put to use, in order to show that the punishment about to be given was approved of by the Church.

◀THE SALEM WITCHES

As two anxious suspects face the court, witnesses point hysterically at them declaring they can see a flock of yellow birds around their heads. This engraving of 1892 captures some of the atmosphere of the Salem witch trials of 1692 in Massachusetts. Several young girls of the town claimed that they had been bewitched by a West Indian slave. This was the only occasion in which the USA experienced the same kind of witch hunting frenzy that had gripped Europe.

▲ COTTON MATHER

The Reverend Cotton Mather, a Massachusetts minister, was one of the leading supporters of the Salem witch trials. After the trials he published a pamphlet justifying the hysteria, entitled *The Wonders of the Invisible World*. Mather was a highly educated and respected man. The fact that such a man could believe in the witches of Salem shows the attitudes and prejudices of the times.

BURNED AT THE STAKE ▶

Most witches were executed by being burned at the stake. The punishment was intended as a taste of the flames of hell that were to come. In this German engraving of 1555, an evil spirit has already come to claim one of the three witches being burned to death. To the right of the picture lies a dead child. Perhaps the women were accused of bringing about his death by evil magic. In the distance an executioner prepares to behead another witch. Beheading was at least a quicker, less agonizing way to die. Witches were also hanged on the gallows, another death that could be slow and horribly painful.

▲ ROUGH JUSTICE

Four unfortunate prisoners, wearing robes and hats designed to humiliate them, sit before the court, accused of witchcraft and heresy. All four were almost certainly tortured to obtain the confessions used as evidence against them. This painting is by the Spanish artist Goya and is entitled *A Scene from the Inquisition*. The Inquisition was set up in 1233 to enforce the authority of the Catholic Church and to prevent the spread of alternative beliefs. Any threat, real or imagined, was dealt with ruthlessly. The Inquisition claimed hundreds of thousands of victims.

▲ MAKING HIM TALK

A woodcut of the 1400s shows a suspect being prepared for a method of torture called strappado. With his hands tied behind his back, he will be suspended from a chain with a weight tied to his feet. Three clerks sit at a table ready to record his confession, while another official addresses him.

◀ LAST CONVICTION

Jane Wenham of Hertford was the last person to be convicted of witchcraft in England. At her trial in 1712, she was sentenced to death. The judge at the trial had no intention of sending her to the gallows, and requested a pardon from Queen Anne. The pardon was granted, but Jane Wenham had to be hidden from an angry mob which had gathered to kill her themselves.

A Magic Seal

Throughout history, seals have been used to fasten things that should not be opened, such as the door of a tomb, or a secret message. Seals were believed to have magic powers from the special inscriptions and symbols that were moulded or etched on to them, and for this reason they were used to ward off evil magic. In this project, a wax-like seal is used to secure a letter written on a scroll. The symbols on the seal come from the art of alchemy, in which men would try to discover a magical formula to turn ordinary metals into gold. The box opposite shows what they represent.

1 Take a lump of self-hardening clay and place it on a work board. Use a rolling pin to roll out the clay to about 10cm x 10cm and 0.75cm thick.

2 Measure the circumference and half the length of an empty tube of sweets. Then cut a slab from the clay to the same measurements.

You will need: self-hardening clay, work board, rolling pin, ruler, small empty sweet tube (or similar) cut in half, modelling tool (or blunt knife), small dish, PVA glue, glue brush, craft knife, red oven-bake modelling material, thick dark ribbon.

4 Use the modelling tool to draw alchemical symbols in the clay inside the circle. Make light marks, so that you can change the design if you want to.

5 When you are happy with your design, go over it again with the modelling tool, making heavier marks. Keep your design as neat as possible.

6 Very carefully turn the slab over. Then spread glue all over the card tube. Roll the clay slab around the tube, taking care not to smudge the design.

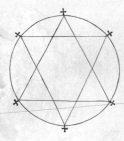

These two ancient star-shaped symbols were frequently used to ward off evil. The six-pointed star on the left is called a hexagram and is also known as the Seal of Solomon or the Star of David. The star on the right is called a pentagram, meaning that it has five points.

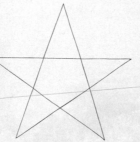

9 Roll the dry clay tube over the red tablet, so that the alchemy symbols leave a good imprint. If the print is uneven, smooth over the tablet and repeat.

10 Use the modelling tool to trim away any excess clay outside the imprinted circle. Bake it in an oven, following the instructions on the packet.

3 Take a small circular dish that fits neatly inside the area of the slab you have cut. Press the dish gently into the clay to leave a circular impression.

ALCHEMY SYMBOLS

☉ Sun = gold

☿ Mercury = mercury

♂ Mars = iron

♄ Saturn = lead

☾ Moon = silver

♀ Venus = copper

♃ Jupiter = tin

Alchemists used these astrological symbols in their secret writings to represent different metals.

7 Use a craft knife to trim away any excess clay. Use your fingers to smooth over the join where the ends of the clay meet. Put to one side to dry thoroughly.

8 Take some red oven-bake modelling material and put it on the board. Use your hands to squash and roll it into a circular tablet shape.

In the past, seals for letters were made of red wax. Molten wax was poured on to the letter and the seal pressed into the wax to leave an impression.

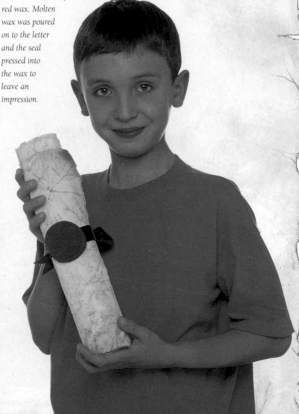

11 Leave the seal to cool. Spread a narrow strip of glue on the back of the seal and stick it in the middle of a piece of thick ribbon. Leave to dry.

12 Use the seal to secure an important piece of paper you want to keep, such as a letter. Roll the paper into a scroll and tie the seal around the middle.

Shamans and Magic

Many people all over the world live in tribal communities. A tribe is a group of people who often share common ancestors and a common territory and culture. Most tribal peoples have healers called shamans, who play an important role in their society. Shamans are also known as witch doctors or medicine men. Many shamans are men, but sometimes women fulfil this role.

Shamans have been highly valued members of tribal societies for more than 30,000 years, and this early existence may be the first ever indication of organized religion. Some shamans have a guardian spirit that is the source of their power. They go into a trance-like state, in which they can communicate with spirits and draw on their enormous power.

Shamans from different tribes share a great many similarities with each other in their abilities and their ways of working. The shaman uses his or her power to heal members of the tribe who are ill. Rituals which involve music and dance, and eating and drinking, are used to see into the future and to bring prosperity to the tribe – for instance, by ensuring that hunting expeditions are successful.

▲ FALSE FACE MASK
Shamans from the Iroquois tribe, of the east coast of North America, wore elaborately painted wood and horsehair masks in ceremonial dances. The wearers took on the power of the spirits that the masks represented, during healing rituals. They believed the mask offered them a way to enter the spirit world and of identifying with spirits.

OLD BEAR ▶
Old Bear was a shaman of the Mandan people of the Great Plains in the USA. This painting of him is the work of the American artist George Caitlin in 1832. In Old Bear's hands are two wand-like batons, decorated with feathers and furs. He also carries healing herbs tucked into the animal hide tied around his middle. The Mandan tribe and their culture were almost wiped out by a smallpox epidemic five years after this painting was completed.

◀ ZULU WITCH DOCTOR
A female Zulu witch doctor from South Africa is working as an oracle, predicting the future with the aid of her spirit helpers. Belief in the magic of shamans and witch doctors is extremely strong in some parts of the world. In their healing roles, witch doctors use their power to diagnose and cure disease.

▲ SUMMONING DRUM

Music and rhythm are an important part of
shamanic rituals. Drums and rattles are used by many tribes.
This leather and wooden drum was used by the Magar tribe of
Nepal. The sound of the music is believed to summon the spirit guardians and
guides of the shaman, and also helps the shaman enter a trance in order to
communicate with the spirits.

▲ ABORIGINAL HEALER

An Aboriginal (native) Australian medicine man of the
1900s has decorated his body with magical markings.
The Aborigines believe that serious illness is sometimes
caused by bad magic. Someone becomes ill because an
invisible spear or stone is thrust into them, leaving a
splinter or bone that will kill them. The medicine man
is called on to extract this splinter or bone. Aboriginal
medicine men are also believed to be able to see and
speak to the spirit doubles of people. If someone is
murdered, a medicine man visits the scene of the crime,
speaks to the dead body's spirit, and names the culprit.

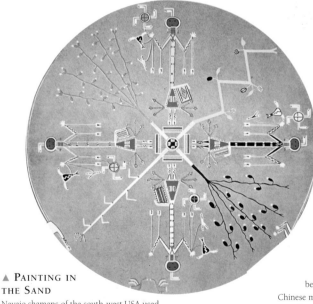

▲ PAINTING IN
THE SAND

Navajo shamans of the south-west USA used
coloured sands to create pictures on the floor of a patient's home.
The paintings showed powerful spirits from Navajo myths and
played a vital role in healing rituals. During the ceremonies, the
patient would sit within the painting while the shaman
summoned spirit powers with sacred chants, and asked them to
cure the patient. After the ritual, the painting was destroyed.

MEDICINE
MAN ▶

Carrying the tools of
his trade and his
bedding on his back, this
Chinese medicine man walks the
footpaths of the Himalayas,
looking for business. He may have
various animal parts for sale,
including bones, shells, skulls,
horns and claws. They may be
used for healing, or as lucky
charms to ward off bad spirits.

A Shaman's Mask

From North America to Africa and Asia, many tribal rituals involve the wearing of elaborate masks, often as part of a ceremonial dance. These are intended to enable the wearer to identify and communicate with particular spirits.

The mask in this project is based on an original one used by shamans in Sri Lanka. The original mask was made out of wood and is supposed to represent a serpent demon called Garayaka. This dangerous demon is said to cause illnesses and is driven from the body of the patient in a purification ritual conducted by the shaman.

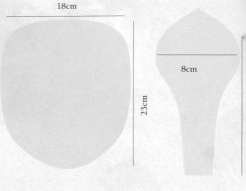

18cm

23cm

8cm

1 Shown above are templates for the main part of the mask and the cobras. You will need three cobras.

You will need: *ruler, white card, black felt-tipped pen, scissors, pencil, masking tape, pair of compasses, newspaper, small mixing bowl, spoon, flour, water, fine sandpaper, thick paintbrushes, white emulsion paint, black, red, orange, yellow and white acrylic paints, fine paintbrushes, thin elastic.*

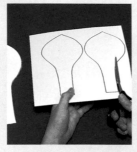

5 Using a pencil and ruler, copy the cobra head template three times on to white card. Follow the measurements shown on the template. Cut out the shapes.

6 Use masking tape or sticky tape to attach the cobra heads to the top of the mask. Gently bend the heads forwards, like a real cobra's head.

7 Use a pair of compasses to draw two circles 12cm across on to card. Draw a circle 2cm across in the middle. Cut out both large circles, then cut out the centre circles.

12 When the papier-mâché is dry, smooth it down with fine sandpaper. Then use a thick paintbrush to apply white emulsion paint all over the mask.

13 When the paint is completely dry, use a pencil to draw in the features of the face. Draw patterns on the ears and cobra heads, too.

14 Paint the mask as shown. Use a thick paintbrush to paint big blocks of colour. Use a fine paintbrush for finer details, such as the teeth and the scales.

15 When the paint is dry, make a hole on either side of the mask. Pass a length of elastic through from the back of each hole and knot at the front.

2 Using a ruler and a black felt-tipped pen, measure and mark out a basic mask shape on to a piece of white card. Use the template shown in step 1.

3 Use a pair of scissors to carefully cut around the shape of the shaman's mask. Try to keep the shape as smooth as possible.

4 Hold the mask up to your face and make marks with a pencil where your eyes and nose are. Now draw the nose and eye shapes in place and cut them out.

A beautifully carved and painted mask from Mongolia represents the Spirit of the Barren Mountain. It is used in a sacred dance that was probably first performed by shamans.

8 Use tape to fix the card circles to either side of the mask to make a pair of ears. Make sure the pieces touch but do not overlap the face.

9 Scrunch up newspaper into long sausage shapes for the mouth and eyebrows. Scrunch up two newspaper balls for the eyeballs. Tape in place.

10 To make the nose, draw a fat triangular shape on to card and cut it out. Make a crease down the middle, then tape it in position on the mask.

11 Mix a paste of flour and water in a bowl into a thick batter. Dip newspaper strips in the paste. Cover the mask in about three layers of papier-mâché.

Shamans wear costumes and masks in rituals to help them to take on the characters of the spirits more fully. The three snake's heads on this particular mask represent the serpent demon that the shaman is trying to drive away.

Fairy-tale Magic

It is through fairy tales, myths and legends that our images of witches and wizards are formed. From the earliest times, right through to the latest films and computer games, witches and wizards continue to capture people's imagination. Most of these stories show witches as people to be feared and avoided. In earlier times, fables about them would have added to the hostility felt towards witchcraft. In recent times, witches have become more friendly figures. The child-eating, cackling monsters of fairy tale have been replaced by good natured softies such as Jan Pienkowski's Meg and her cat Mog.

Wizards, however, have never attracted the same hostility as witches. From figures such as Merlin at the court of King Arthur, to Gandalf in Tolkien's *The Lord of the Rings*, wizards have almost always been heroes. The Harry Potter books by J K Rowling, with their comical and exciting stories of children training to be wizards and witches, are far from the cruel images of earlier times.

▲ **DR FAUSTUS**
Dr Faustus, inside a magic circle with spell book in hand, summons a demon. In the story, Faustus sells his soul to the Devil in exchange for 24 years of unlimited wisdom and pleasure. As the year of his damnation draws nearer, however, Faustus grows increasingly fearful. On the night the Devil comes to claim his soul, a fierce wind swirls around his house. His neighbours hear terrified screams. In the morning they find his crumpled body in a dung heap, and his brains, teeth, eyeballs and blood splattered over the walls.

◄ **MACBETH**
Surrounded by malevolent crows, three hags prepare to meet the hero of William Shakespeare's play *Macbeth*. In the play, the Scottish lord, Macbeth, is confronted by the witches on his travels and they predict that he is destined to be King of Scotland. Great tragedy and bloodshed follow, and Macbeth is eventually killed. Shakespeare included the witches to appeal to King James I, who was interested in witchcraft. To mention the play's name in a theatre is said to bring bad luck.

▲ **A SLEEPING SPELL**
In the story *Sleeping Beauty*, a beautiful princess is cursed by a witch. She pricks her finger on the witch's spindle, sending her into an charmed sleep. She is unable to wake up until a handsome prince comes to the rescue and wakes her with a kiss. Many old folk tales such as this were retold by two German brothers called Jacob and Wilhelm Grimm. Their stories, published in the 1800s, were tremendously popular all over the world, and are still told to children today.

BLACK CATS AND BROOMSKICKS ▶

Some of the most charming and atmospheric children's book illustrations were done by an artist called Arthur Rackham in the early 1900s. His illustrations for *Ingoldsby Legends* show the classic image of witches with pointed hats, broomsticks and black cats. *Ingoldsby Legends* was a collection of country tales and medieval legends written in the mid-1800s by a clergyman called Richard Harris Barham.

▲ INTO THE INK

This illustration shows a famous magician called Agrippa punishing three naughty boys by plunging them into an inkwell. It appears in a book of cautionary tales by the German writer Heinrich Hoffman, published in 1876. In the book, children who misbehave come to a gruesome end. Agrippa was a real person. He was a scholar in the 1500s who wrote books on magic. He was said to be a sorcerer and to practise black magic.

◀ BABA YAGA

The Russian witch Baba Yaga, shown here riding her broomstick, loved to roast and eat people, especially children. Baba Yaga lived in a house in the woods, which was ringed with stakes topped with human skulls. The house was built on chicken and dogs' legs, and could turn around at her command. This illustration comes from a British children's book published in 1915 called *Old Peter's Russian Tales*.

◀ HANSEL AND GRETEL

A crucial scene from *Hansel and Gretel*, a German fairy tale retold by the Grimm brothers, shows Gretel pushing a wicked witch into an oven. In the story, Hansel and Gretel become lost in the woods. They come across an odd gingerbread house and are tempted inside by a peculiar, but kindly, old lady. Alas, their host is a witch who intends to eat them for her supper. Due to Gretel's quick actions, the children manage to escape.

Screen Witches

Cinema is a wonderful way of telling a scary story. In a darkened room and with a hushed, expectant audience, a visit to the movies is a spellbinding experience. Not surprisingly, witches have always been popular subjects and have fascinated film makers and audiences throughout the history of cinema. Films, such as the 1922 Swedish film *Witchcraft Through the Ages* and *The Blair Witch Project* of 1999, which made a big impact when they were released, were designed to thrill and horrify.

As in the images from myths and legends, witches in films and television are either shown as sinister, ugly, old crones as in *Snow White and the Seven Dwarfs*, or as beautiful and determined, as in Samantha from the popular TV series *Bewitched*. Whatever they look like, all these witches have the ability to work magic for good or evil. The image of witches is gradually becoming more positive. The modern-day equivalents of the hags that our ancestors believed worked evil magic in our midst are more likely to be kindly rather than frightening characters.

▲ A POISONED APPLE

Snow White looks on suspiciously as a warty old woman tries to tempt her with a poisonous apple. Walt Disney's 1937 film is a cartoon adaptation of a Grimms' fairy tale. Disney described the witch as a mixture of William Shakespeare's Lady Macbeth and the big bad wolf from *Little Red Riding Hood*. More than 60 years on, she still has the power to frighten people. The witch is really Snow White's stepmother, the wicked queen, who has disguised herself by a spell.

I MARRIED A WITCH ▶

Despite the pointed hat, black cape and broomstick, American film star Veronica Lake fails to look sinister and ugly in the 1942 film, *I Married a Witch*. She plays a witch who has come back to life to seek revenge on a politician whose ancestors had her burned at the stake.

▲ BLOCKBUSTER

The 1939 version of *The Wizard of Oz* was the most successful of three films based on L Frank Baum's children's novel. The heroine Dorothy (played in the 1939 version by Judy Garland) is swept away in a tornado, and lands in the fantasy land of Oz, where she is tormented by the Wicked Witch of the North. She makes friends and has many adventures with the Scarecrow, the Tin Man and the Cowardly Lion.

▲ MERLIN THE MAGICIAN

In the 1981 film *Excalibur*, a version of the legend of King Arthur, Nicol Williamson played court magician Merlin. He battles with Arthur's half-sister and enemy, Morgan le Fay. Williamson, seen here wearing a steel skull cap, instead of the more traditional pointed wizard hat, portrays Merlin as a bustling, eccentric figure. The film was based on Sir Thomas Malory's book *Morte d'Arthur*.

▲ THE WITCHES

American actress Anjelica Huston is unrecognizable beneath her grotesque make-up. She played a wicked witch in the 1990 film of Roald Dahl's book *The Witches*. In the film, the witch plans to poison all the children in Britain with a powerful magic potion. Only a little boy (who has been turned into a mouse) and his granny can stop her evil intentions. Like many of Dahl's stories, the film is dark and menacing but also very humorous.

▲ BEWITCHED

Elizabeth Montgomery played the witch Samantha in the American TV series *Bewitched*, which was first screened from 1964 to 1972. One of TV's classic comedies, the series has been shown in many different countries around the world. Samantha was married to a down-to-earth husband, Darrin, who disapproved of his wife using her magic powers. Samantha famously twitched her nose to work her spells. As often as not, she used her powers to put right the muddle left behind by her meddling family. Still popular today, *Bewitched* was originally inspired by the film *I Married a Witch*.

◄ GANDALF THE WIZARD

In 1978, J R R Tolkien's classic trilogy of books, *The Lord of the Rings*, was made into a film. The part of Gandalf the wizard (shown here in a poster for the film) was played by American actor William Squire. The film, which is a mixture of animation and live action, covers only the first two parts of the trilogy. It is the story of a band of travellers who seek to defeat an evil sorcerer and his armies with the aid of a powerful, but evil, magic ring.

A Hallowe'en Feast

Hallowe'en, on October 31st, is the night most closely associated with witchcraft. In pre-Christian times, this was when the beginning of winter was celebrated. Hallowe'en's association with witches stems from the legend that the sun is so low in the sky on that day that the gates of the underworld have to be opened to let in the light. As the gates open, demons and spectres slip out to plague the Earth.

In the USA, the ritual of "trick or treat" takes place on Hallowe'en. Children dressed as witches and ghouls visit houses, demanding food or drink. In return they promise not to play a prank on the person they visit. In this project, you can find out how to make some scary food for a Hallowe'en party.

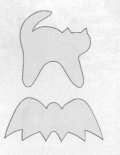

1 Scale up these two templates on to thick card and cut out. You could also make other shapes, such as jack-o'-lanterns and ghosts.

2 Put 110g butter or margarine in a mixing bowl. Add 110g caster sugar. Stir with a wooden spoon until the mixture is fluffy and creamy.

For the cat and bat biscuits you will need : card, pencil, scissors, mixing bowl, butter, caster sugar, wooden spoon, 1 egg, flour, black food colouring, chopping board, rolling pin, blunt knife, baking tray, wire rack, red and green icing.

For the potato face you will need: 1 large potato, spoon, mixing bowl, green food colouring, butter, grated cheese, salt, pepper, chopping board, 1 carrot, 1 red pepper, salad onions, 1 cooked sausage, sliced mushrooms, salad cress, a handful of grated orange cheese.

For the drink you will need: paintbrush, PVA glue, coloured plastic straws, toy spiders, tall drinking glass, small plate, ice cream, fizzy drink, chocolate flakes.

These biscuits would make an excellent treat for trick or treating on Hallowe'en. This custom recalls days long gone when people were wary of offending local witches in case the witch placed a curse upon them.

3 Cut the carrot into strips. Cut the red pepper in a zigzag for teeth. Cut the ends of the onions into fan shapes. Slice the sausage. Fry the mushrooms in butter.

4 Use the vegetables and sausage to make a face and hair on the potato. Sprinkle grated orange cheese around the potato face to make it even more tasty.

1 For the drink: Use the paintbrush to put a dab of glue near the top of each plastic straw. Fix a toy spider firmly in place on to each straw.

2 Put the glass on a small plate. Put 3 or 4 tablespoons of ice cream in the glass. (Chocolate mint chip looks good, because it is a ghoulish green colour.)

3 Add 1 beaten egg, 270g flour and a few drops of black food colouring. Mix until it forms a dough. Stir really well so that the food colouring blends in.

4 Roll the dough out on a board to about 1cm thick. Place the bat and cat templates on the dough and carefully cut around them with a blunt knife.

5 Roll out the leftover dough again and cut out more shapes. Place the animal shapes on a non-stick baking tray. Bake for 20 minutes at 190°C/250°F/Gas 5.

6 When the shapes are cooked, remove from the oven and cool on a wire rack. Mix up red and green icing. Use your fingers to add the bats' and cats' features.

1 Ask an adult to bake a large potato. When it has cooled a bit, use a knife to cut off the top. Use a spoon to scoop the insides into a bowl. Add green colouring.

2 Add 50g butter, 50g grated cheese and season with salt and pepper. Mix with a fork. Spoon the mixture back in the potato skin and keep warm.

3 Pour fizzy drink over the ice cream. Limeade works well because it is ghastly green, like the ice cream. Pour in enough so that it really froths up.

4 Sprinkle little flakes of chocolate over the top. You could add mini marshmallows or hundreds and thousands instead. Stick the straws into the drink.

With these delicious treats, your party is bound to go with a bang. Make enough biscuits, potato faces and ghoulish drinks for everyone you have invited. Don't forget to decorate the room with some suitably scary trimmings.

After the Witch Hunts

All crazes eventually die down, and witch hunting was no different. As the 1700s dawned, the persecutions that had claimed so many lives over the previous 300 years, gradually began to grind to a halt. In England, the last witch was convicted in 1712, but was given a royal pardon. In Scotland, a witch was burned in 1727. There were some executions in France in 1745, and finally, in Bavaria in 1775, the last witch to be executed in Europe was beheaded.

The witch hunts had brought terrible turmoil, and whole communities had been devastated, but times were changing. Science was in fashion and an era that became known as the Age of Reason arrived. As the 1700s passed, the feudal societies of Europe began to modernize themselves. There was a general drift in population from countryside to town. In the 1800s, a world of roads and railways, cities and factories began to take shape. However, interest in magic is still present in modern Western society, and many people practise different versions of magic and witchcraft. Today, witchcraft involves honouring the earth and nature and is a far cry from the witchcraft imagined by the Christian Church during the witch-hunts.

▲ HANDFAST CEREMONY

A bridal couple celebrate their marriage in a modern witchcraft ceremony. They are taking part in a ritual known as handfasting. The couple have made a colourful, three-strand fibre band that binds them together. The three strands stand for the bride, the groom and their relationship. If, in later life, the couple decide to separate, the union can be undone in another witchcraft ceremony called handparting.

◄ LOCKED IN THE PILLORIES

In the 1700s and 1800s, people were still prosecuted for witchcraft, but they were more likely to be guilty of trickery and preying on vulnerable people. Their fate was not the stake or gallows. Instead, they were locked up in a public place in a pillory or stocks (in which feet were locked). Then they were a target for any passer-by who felt like pelting them with rotten fruit and vegetables.

TALKING TO THE DEAD ►

In the late 1800s, spiritualism became fashionable. This is a belief that people can communicate with the spirits of the dead at a gathering called a seance. At this seance in New York in 1887, a guitar somehow floats in the air, although everyone present is holding hands. Spiritualism continued to be immensely popular in the early 1900s, particularly after World War I. Widows, mothers and children were desperate to make contact with the millions of soldiers who had died in the war.

MODERN MAGICIAN ▶

English magician Aleister Crowley poses dramatically for the camera, dressed in ceremonial robes and surrounded by the ritual implements of his magic. Crowley had a curious career. Hounded by Britain's popular newspapers, which described him as the wickedest man alive, he died a drug addict in 1947. He remains a fascinating and even honoured figure, however, to those who practise magic today. He wrote more than 100 books on the subject and his motto, "Do what thou wilt, shall be the whole of the law", has been adopted as a way of life by many modern magicians.

◀ THE FATHER OF MODERN WITCHCRAFT

Gerald Gardner is sometimes called the Father of Modern Witchcraft. For many years Gardner was a British government worker employed as a plantation manager in South-east Asia. In 1939 he returned to England and claimed to have been initiated into a secret group called the Wicca. In fact, he probably created modern witchcraft. The witchcraft laws were abolished in 1951, and in 1954 Gardner published a book about Wicca (modern witchcraft) called *Witchcraft Today*. This and his other books were tremendously influential. They formed the idea of the witch as someone who practised a pre-Christian religion.

TOOLS OF WITCHCRAFT ▼

Those who practise witchcraft today use tools and objects in their spells and rituals. Here you can see two of them. The chalice is a feminine symbol. It holds wine or water. The knife, or athame, is a masculine symbol which is used to direct psychic energy.

◀ INITIATION CEREMONY

Modern-day witches are forming a magic circle as part of an initiation ceremony. Because the term witchcraft has such bad associations for many people, they prefer to use the term Wicca (an old English word meaning witch) to describe their activities. Today, Wiccan groups can be found all over the world, especially in Europe, North America, Australia and Japan.

Timeline

Magic has been part of human culture since society began, and it still plays an important role in some societies today. Over the centuries, attitudes towards witches have changed. One of the most disturbing periods in history was between 1450 and 1700, when witches were feared and violently persecuted.

Before 3000BC

30,000BC POSSIBLY the first evidence of tribal shamans found in cave paintings and archaeological remains.

3000–1000BC ANCIENT Egyptian civilization flourished. Magic spells and rituals are part of everyday life.

prehistoric cave painting, possibly of a shaman, from France

3000BC PALM READING first practised in China.

2000BC–AD100

2000–146BC ANCIENT GREEK civilization flourishes. Many legends from Greece concerning witchcraft, such as shape changing, familiars and horned gods, will become part of Western European folklore.

500BC ALCHEMY BEGINS in Ancient China.

c.AD100 THE TRADITIONAL text of the Old Testament is translated into Greek by Jewish authorities. In it are the words "Thou shall not suffer a witch to live". This phrase is used by later Christians to justify their persecution of witches.

AD100–800 MISSIONARIES convert Europe from pagan religions to Christianity.

1400–1431

c. 1400s A FRENCH illustration shows the first known images of witches flying on broomsticks.

1404–1440 LIFE OF GILLES de Rais, one of the most notorious sorcerers and alchemists who lived in the Middle Ages.

French illustration of a witch flying on a broomstick

1428 HERETIC trials in the Dauphine region of France. 167 people burned at stake over next 20 years.

1431 JOAN OF ARC burned as a heretic.

1450–1484

c. 1450 BEGINNING OF mass persecution of witches in Europe.

1459 WITCH TRIALS in Arras, France. Hundreds implicated as mass hysteria grips the town.

1473–1541 LIFE OF PARACELSUS, the famous Swiss alchemist and medical scientist.

1484 POPE INNOCENT VIII issues a papal bull used to authorize witch hunting in Germany.

Christian cross

1485–1503

c. 1485 SIR THOMAS MALORY writes *Morte d'Arthur* – tales of the legendary King Arthur.

1486 *MALLEUS MALEFICARUM* (Hammer of Witches) published. It was a witch judge's manual and was hostile to women.

c. 1500 RELIGIOUS RIVALRY and warfare in Europe inspire greater persecution of witches.

alchemical symbols

1503–1566 LIFE of Nostradamus, French healer and astrologer.

1591–1604

1591 NICOLAS REMY is chief prosecutor of witches in Lorraine, France. He sends over 900 to be executed.

1597 JAMES VI OF SCOTLAND's *Demonology* published It hardens prejudice against witchcraft in England.

1603–1606 300 PEOPLE sent to be burned as witches in Fulda, south Germany, by infamous judge Balthasar Ross.

1603–1625 REIGN OF JAMES I of England and James VI of Scotland.

1604 CHRISTOPHER MARLOWE's famous play *Dr Faustus* performed.

1606–1620

1606 SHAKESPEARE'S PLAY *Macbeth* features the three most famous witches in literature.

1609 PIERRE DE LANCRE, chief prosecutor in South-west France claims 30,000 people in his district are witches. He also says 100,000 people attend sabbats in Bordeaux. He sends 600 suspects to their deaths.

1618–1648 THE THIRTY YEARS War rages in central Europe. Witch hunting at its height.

1620s 900 PEOPLE BURNED as witches in Würzburg, Germany.

witch's hex doll, used for spell making

1625–1727

c. 1625 600 MEN AND WOMEN burned as witches at Bamburg, Germany.

1626 *COMPENDIUM MALEFICARUM* (Handbook of Witches) published. It does much to fan the flames of witch hunting hysteria.

1631 FRIEDRICH VON SPEE publishes *Cautio Criminalis* (Precautions for Prosecutors) in Germany, opposing witch hunt hysteria.

1642–1727 LIFE OF SIR ISAAC Newton – Britain's most distinguished scientist and alchemist.

Newton's famous book on the laws of motion

1812–1821

1812–1822 THE BROTHERS GRIMM fairy tales are published in three volumes. They contain several stories concerning witches, which introduce future generations of children to the images of a witch as a crooked-nosed, warty-faced evil old hag.

a witch's cat from a fairy tale

1817–1821 A POLTERGEIST supposedly persecutes the Bell family in Tennessee, USA. One of the family is killed. People believed in evil magic at the time, so the ghost became known as the Bell Witch.

1850–1922

c. 1850 SPIRITUALISM becomes popular, in which people try to contact the souls of their dead friends and relatives.

1875–1947 LIFE OF MAGICIAN Aleister Crowley. He achieves a reputation in the newspapers as the wickedest man alive.

1883–1964 LIFE OF GERALD GARDNER. Considered to be the father of modern witchcraft.

1922 THE SWEDISH FILM *Witchcraft through the Ages* is made. A silent horror film, it is banned for many years.

ritual objects of modern witchcraft

1937–1950

1937 DISNEY releases *Snow White*, an animated film of the well-known Grimm's fairy tale.

1939 THE FILM of *The Wizard of Oz* is released, based on writer L. Frank Baum's popular novel of fantasy adventure.

1937–1955 J.R.R. TOLKIEN publishes his fantasy novels, *The Hobbit* and the *Lord of the Rings* trilogy, featuring the kindly wizard Gandalf.

astrological symbols

AD367–550

AD367 FIRST ORGANIZED witch hunt by Emperor Valerian in Rome.

AD391 CHRISTIANITY BECOMES the official religion of the Roman Empire.

c. AD450 LIFE OF THE legendary Arthur King of Britain, who was aided by his court magician Merlin.

AD476 FALL OF ROME. Pagan and Christian practices continue to co-exist in Europe.

c. AD550 LEGEND of Greek monk Theophilus, who sells his soul to the Devil. This story will become well known as *Dr Faustus*.

AD550–1174

c. AD750 ALCHEMICAL IDEAS reach the Middle East from China and India.

AD787 EMPEROR CHARLEMAGNE issues decree calling for the execution of anyone discovered making sacrifices to the Devil.

c. 1050 CONTACT WITH ARAB countries brings alchemical ideas to Europe.

1174 HENRY II OF ENGLAND's wife Eleanor suspected of practising witchcraft.

a witch burned at the stake

1193–1324

1193–1280 LIFE OF BISHOP Albertus Magnus, scientist and student of magic.

1233 CATHOLIC CHURCH founds the Inquisition to persecute heretics.

1320 FAILED ASSASSINATION attempt on Pope John XXII said to involve poisoning and witchcraft. Persecution of heretics by church intensifies.

1323 MAGICIAN BURNED alive in Paris.

1324 PETRONILA DE MEATH is first person condemned to be burned in Ireland.

1520s–1536

1520s SPANISH EXPLORER Cabez de Vaca witnesses Native North American shamans curing the sick.

1527 BIRTH OF JOHN DEE, Alchemist, Sorcerer and Astrologer to the court of Queen Elizabeth I of England.

necklace used by a Native North American shaman

1532 CAROLINA CODE issued in Germany. Imposes torture and death for witchcraft.

1536 ANNE BOLEYN, wife of King Henry VIII of England, is executed. Henry ruined her reputation by accusing her of witchcraft, among other things.

1555–1565

1555 NOSTRADAMUS publishes *Centuries* – his famous predictions.

1562 CATHOLIC CHURCH announces intention to win back Germany from Protestantism at Council of Trent. Persecution of witches intensifies.

1563 ELIZABETH I of England passes statute against witchcraft.

1565 THE FIRST WITCHCRAFT trial in England takes place against three women from Chelmsford. Two of them are hanged.

1576–1590

1576–1612 REIGN OF RUDOLF II, Holy Roman Emperor and patron of alchemists in Prague.

1585 REGINALD SCOTT's book *The Discoverie of Witchcraft* attempts to discredit witch hunting. It has very little affect on attitudes.

1589 133 WITCHES BURNED in a single day in Quedlinburg in Saxony.

1590 NORTH BERWICK witches of Scotland accused of trying to kill James VI.

witches in company with the Devil

1645–1684

1645–6 WITCHFINDER GENERAL Matthew Hopkins conducts his witch hunts in eastern England. He is discredited and dies within a year.

1647 MATTHEW HOPKINS publishes a booklet entitled *Discovery of Witchcraft* shortly before his death, to try to justify his witch hunts.

1669 85 WITCHES BURNED at Mora, Sweden.

1669 ALCHEMIST HENNIG BRAND accidently discovers the chemical phosphorus.

1684 ALICE MOLLAND is the last woman to be executed as a witch in England.

1692–1727

1692 SALEM WITCH TRIALS, the most infamous outbreak of witch hunting in North America. The trials result in 19 executions.

1700s GREATER SCIENTIFIC KNOWLEDGE and changing social conditions lead to a decline in the belief in witchcraft, and persecution gradually stops.

1712 JANE WENHAM is the last witch to be convicted in English court. She is given a royal pardon.

1727 JANET HORNE is the last witch to be executed in Scotland.

a witch is punished in a pillory

1736–1787

1736 NEW LAWS IN ENGLAND remove penalties for witchcraft and replace them with punishments for fraudulent fortune-telling, and other hoaxes relating to the practice of magic.

1745 FATHER LOUIS DEBARAZ is the last witch to be executed in France.

1775 ANNA MARIA SCHWAGEL of Bavaria is the last witch to be executed in Europe.

1787 ALL WITCHCRAFT laws in Austria repealed.

1951–1976

1951 WITCHCRAFT LAWS repealed in Britain, and witchcraft is now legal. Revival of witchcraft as a kind of pagan religion in Britain, the USA, and other parts of the world.

1964 CLASSIC COMEDY SERIES *Bewitched* is first screened on American TV. It is subsequently shown in many different countries all over the world.

1976 THE WORLD HEALTH Organization recommends that witch doctors join medical teams in Africa.

African shaman performing a healing ritual

1996–1999

1996 POPULAR TV COMEDY *Sabrina the Teenage Witch* is first screened on American TV.

1997 J.K. ROWLING publishes the first of the Harry Potter series of books *Harry Potter and the Philosopher's Stone*. The book becomes a worldwide phenomenal success.

1999 THE BLAIR WITCH PROJECT becomes the most profitable film ever made. Fascination in witches is as strong as ever.

the pentagram – a magic symbol

2000–

2000 J.K. ROWLING publishes the fourth in the Harry Potter series of books, *Harry Potter and the Goblet of Fire*. It becomes one of the most successful books ever.

SHAMANISM is still practised in many places around the world, such as Nepal, Indonesia and Aboriginal Australia.

Aboriginal shaman

GLOSSARY

alchemy
The art of trying to turn base (ordinary) metals, such as lead, into precious ones, such as silver or gold. Alchemists also tried to find the secret of everlasting life.

amulet
An object believed to have magical properties and the ability to protect someone or something against evil.

astrology
The art of studying the stars and planets in order to foretell the future.

black magic
The art of causing harm through magic.

Catholic Church
A branch of the Christian Church, governed by the Pope in Rome.

cauldron
A large metal pot, supposedly used by witches to brew their spells. A symbol of female energy in modern witchcraft.

charm
An object or a saying believed to have magical powers.

Christianity
The belief that there is one god, whose son Jesus Christ came to Earth to save humankind.

curse
A magical act carried out in order to harm or trouble someone.

demon
An evil spirit.

Devil
The most evil being, and enemy of God. Also known as Satan.

Devil's Marks
Marks on the body, such as scars or moles, said to have been put there by the Devil to identify his followers.

divination
Foretelling the future.

Early Modern
The period in European history between 1450 and 1650. It followed the Medieval period, and was the time when witch hunting began.

elixir of life
A substance sought by alchemists that would give them the secret of everlasting life. See also philosopher's stone.

familiar
A spirit that serves a witch, which appears in the shape of an animal, such as a toad.

Hallowe'en
A Christian festival held on 31 October which replaces the old European Samhain. It gets its name from All Hallows (All Saints) Eve, which takes place on 1 November.

heretic
One who practises a heresy – a religious teaching that does not follow the authorized teaching of the Church.

hex doll
A doll used in witchcraft to work a curse or put a spell on a person. Also known as a poppet.

Inquisition
A court of the Catholic Church, set up in 1233, which was responsible for finding heretics and punishing them.

magic
The art of contacting a spirit world.

magician
Someone who practises magic.

mandrake
A plant thought to have magical powers, the root of which was thought to look like a human being.

medicine man or woman
A member of a tribe who heals and helps people through the use of magical rituals. See also witch doctor.

Medieval
A term describing people, events or objects of the Middle Ages.

medium
A person who is thought to have the ability to communicate with the dead.

Middle Ages
The period in European history between 1050 and 1450.

occult
Anything that involves magical, hidden or supernatural forces.

oracle
In ancient Greece or Rome, a priest or a priestess through whom the gods were thought to speak and to foretell the future.

pagan
Someone or something that relates to ancient religions, in which many gods are worshipped.

persecution
The act of finding and punishing members of a certain section of society because of their beliefs, their identity or their actions.

philosopher's stone
A substance sought by alchemists that would help them to turn base (ordinary) metals into gold. See also elixir of life.

propaganda
Information distributed with the intentional aim of influencing people's opinions.

Protestant Church
Any of the branches of the Christian Church that separated themselves from the Catholic Church in the 1500s, during a period known as the Reformation.

ritual
Traditional words and actions that are repeated every time a certain ceremony takes place.

Roman Empire
Large parts of Europe, Africa and Asia, ruled over by the Romans between 27BC and AD476.

sabbat
A ceremony in which witches were said to worship the Devil and perform evil acts.

Satanism
Devil worship.

scrying
Foretelling the future.

shaman
A member of a tribe who uses magic to heal and help people.

shape-shifting
The art of changing shape, said to have been one of the skills of a witch.

sorcerer
Someone who practises magic.

spell
A set of magic words and actions that can be used to influence people and events.

spirit
A being from another realm, either an ancestor or a plant or animal helper.

spiritualism
The practice of talking to the spirit world through a medium.

Stone Age
The period in human history when tools and weapons were made of stone.

supernatural
Any event or occurrence that cannot be explained by science.

tarot cards
A pack of 78 cards designed to tell the future. The first known reference to tarot cards comes from the Middle Ages.

trance
A sleep-like state under which some people are said to be able to communicate with spirits.

trial
A gathering in which a person accused of a crime is found innocent or guilty, depending on the evidence given.

trick or treat
A recent Hallowe'en tradition, which began in the USA, in which children request sweets or small gifts in return for not playing a naughty trick.

warlock
A male witch.

Wicca
A modern, nature-worshipping religion.

wise man or woman
A person who traditionally used magic to heal and help others. Such people were allso known as cunning folk.

witch
Someone, usually a woman, who possesses magical powers and who practises witchcraft.

witch doctor
A man or woman in a tribe who uses magic to heal and help people. See also medicine man or woman.

witch hunt
The act of finding witches in order to punish them.

witchcraft
The art of using magic.

wizard
A man who possesses magical powers, usually used for good purposes.

INDEX

A
Africa 7, 48, 50
Agrippa 53
alchemy 5, 12, 30-1, 32-3
America 5, 6, 42, 43, 48, 49, 50
amulets 10-11
Apollo 9
Apuleius 27
Asia 50
astrology, 20-1, 36-7
Australian Aboriginals 6, 7, 49

B
Bacchus 9
Blackfoot 5
Brand, Hennig 30
burning at the stake 45

C
cards 36, 37
Catholic Church 12, 13, 14, 26, 37, 38, 44
cauldrons 4, 18-19, 36
Celts 7, 9
Cernunnos 9
Chalenas 9
Charles VII of France 13
charms 10, 24-5
China 30, 37, 49
Christianity 4, 12, 18, 42
cinema 54-5
Circe 8
Compendium Maleficarum 14
Crowley, Aleister 59
crystals 25, 36
cunning folk 22, 36

D
dance 7, 9, 38, 48
Dancing Sorcerer 8
Dark Ages 12
de Rais, Gilles 12
Dee, Dr John 15
Devil 12, 14, 19, 26, 38-9
Dionysus 9
Druids 7

E
Egypt, ancient 8, 10, 30

elixir of life 31
Europe 4, 12, 14-15, 16, 18, 32, 38, 42-3

F
fairy tales 52-3, 54-5
familiars 18-19
Faustus, Dr 12, 52
flying 26-7
foxgloves 23
future, forecasting 9, 36-7, 48

G
Gardner, Gerald 58
Gaul 7
Greece, ancient 8, 9, 38

H
Haida 6
Halloween 28, 40, 56-7
healing 6, 8, 12, 22, 23, 49
Henry II of England 13
heresy 12, 32, 42
hex dolls 14, 39
Hopkins, Matthew 43
horned gods 9
Horus 10
human remains 22, 39

I
India 37
Inquisition 45
invisibility 18, 19, 26

J
James I of England 15, 52
Jews 38
Joan of Arc 13

K
Kamchatka 6, 7
Kelly, Edward 15

L
le Fay, Morgan 4, 55
love potions 12, 23

M
Macbeth 22, 52
magic 4, 6, 8, 12, 26, 48-9
magicians 32-3

Magnus, Albertus 13
Malleus Maleficarum 14
mandrakes 23, 27
masks 48-9
Mather, Cotton 44
medicine men and women 5, 48-9
Mephistopheles 12
Merlin 55
Middle Ages 12-13, 30
Middle East 30, 31
Mochica 6
music 7, 48, 49

N
Native Americans: 5, 6, 7, 48-9
Newton, Sir Isaac 31
Nostradamus 37

O
Old Bear 48
oracles 9

P
palm reading 36, 37
Pan 9
Paracelsus 31
persecution 4, 6, 12, 13, 14, 42-3
Pharaohs 10
philosopher's stone 4, 31
phosphorus 30
plants 22, 23
Protestant churches 14, 26, 38, 44
punishment 44-5
Pythia 9

Q
Queen Eleanor 13

R
rhythm 7, 49
rituals 6, 8, 48-9
Rome, ancient 8, 9, 12
roses 23
Rudolf II, Holy Roman Emperor 31
Russia 6, 7

S
sabbat 5, 9, 27, 38-9
sacrifice 8, 9
sailors 23
Salem witch trials 42, 43, 44

sand paintings 49
science 5, 30-1, 58
Scott, Sir Walter 15
scrying 36-7
Shakespeare, William 22
shamans 4, 6, 7, 8, 48-9
shape-shifting 26-7
soothsaying 9
sorcerers 4
spells 5, 22-3
spirits 6, 7, 36, 48, 49
spiritualism 58
stocks 59
Stone Age 8
storms 12, 22, 23

T
Theophilus 12
things to make
    amulet 10-11
    charm bag 24-5
    Halloween lantern 40-1
    Halloween party food 56-7
    magic seal 46-7
    magical decorations 20-1
    shaman's mask 50-1
    witch mobile 28-9
    witch's costume 16-17
    wizard's costume 34-5
Thoth 8
torture 14, 44-5
totem poles 6
trances 7, 9, 26, 36, 48
trials 42-3, 44-5
trick or treat 56

V
Visigoths 12

W
warlocks 4, 5
water 43
weighing 42
Wenham, Jane 45
Wicca 58-9
wise men and women
witch doctors 4, 5, 8, 48-9
witch-hunts 14-15, 42-3
witchcraft through the ages 60-1
witches and wizards 4, 5

Z
Zodiac, signs of 21